CW01513060

Artisan Bread Cookbook

Artisan Bread Baking Recipes for Beginners,

Easy Steps How to Make Healthy and Delicious Bread at Home.

Karla Samadan

contained within this document, including, but not limited to, errors, omissions, or inaccuracies.

Table of Contents

Chapter 4

Chapter 5

Chapter 8

Chapter 9

Introduction

When you walk down a street, even in a city you have never been in before, you will know when there is a bakery nearby. The amazing aromas are mouthwatering and draw you like a bee to flowers. And with good reason, because artisan bread and rolls are simply in a league of their own.

Very often people want to start making their own bread, to create those delicious loaves with crunchy crusts and soft insides they buy. So why don't you start baking, what makes you doubt that you are able to do this?

Overwhelmingly the answer to this boils down to two reasons. Novice bakers are intimidated by the degree of difficulty of making artisan bread. They are very complicated and include multiple steps and they feel that only people who are master bakers can accomplish perfect artisan bread. Yes, there are quite complicated bread recipes, but there are countless easy, and quick recipes that make baking bread fun instead of a chore that leads to frustration.

The second reason is that people are put off by the very lengthy process of baking artisan bread. They see recipes giving rising times of 24 hours and most people simply do not have time for this or have the patience to wait that long.

These are the reasons that are the inspiration for this book. Factual, substantiated information and tried and tested recipes that have at the most 3-4 hours of rising time. All the recipes can be baked with standard equipment found in all kitchens and alternatives given for items that everyone may not have. The whole idea of this book for novice bakers is to show you that it can be done. Yes, you can when you are only starting out on your journey of discovering how much fun you can have baking bread at home. We definitely do not want you to head for the hills in horror and throw your baking pans in the trash. That is why the recipes and methods used are simple, straightforward, and designed to get that bread in and out of the oven in the shortest time possible.

Benefits of Baking Bread at Home

The naysayers are quick to say that it is not viable to bake bread at home in the 21st century, that people don't have the time to waste on this and that it is too complicated. Ignore them and instead look at the many benefits you gain when you bake at home.

- You are in control of what goes into the bread. Every ingredient is your choice to put in and you do not have to resign yourself to eating commercial bread filled with additives we are not happy to put into our bodies.

- Your bread is from the oven directly to the table, absolute freshness is guaranteed and with no preservatives to extend the shelf life of your bread.

- Customization of the recipes as you can add a favorite spice or ingredient to add flavor. You can turn basic recipes into holiday bread with a few tweaks and use your go-to recipes all year round.

- No empty calories from dextrose and corn syrup that is found in the majority of commercial bread. You also are in control of how much sugar you add to a loaf of bread.

- You know that when you bake whole wheat bread that it is 100% whole wheat, and the same goes with any whole grains.

- Most people who are not bakers, don't believe that the actual cost of a loaf of homemade bread is roughly half of the cost of a store-bought loaf of bread. Yet, simple math proves this fact. So, it is definitely cost saving to bake your own bread.

- Commercially baked bread cannot be compared with homemade bread when it comes to taste. Homemade is far superior in taste and flavor.

- A huge health benefit in much lower sodium content than mass-produced bread. On average store-bought bread contains 0.02 oz (½ g) per slice. When you add that up, 6 slices of bread contain half the daily salt intake for an adult. This is very bad news for people with hypertension, so switching to baking low-sodium bread at home is the solution.

- It is easy to cater for any food allergies when you bake your own bread. For people with debilitating food allergies this is critically important. Baking at home means you not only can avoid any allergens, but you also know that whatever equipment you use has not been in contact with an allergen that could harm you.

- Homemade sourdough bread brings several health benefits because most commercially made sourdough bread actually contains standard yeast so does not have the health benefits of the real thing.

  o Sourdough benefits people who are gluten sensitive as the fermentation of sourdough breaks down gluten, making it easier for people to digest.

  o Sourdough lessens the risks of developing diabetes as sourdough is lower on the glycemic index.

  o Sourdough has a natural preservative that is mold-fighting, so the bread stays fresh for much longer without any of the preservatives you find in mass-produced bread.

- Baking at home does take time, but you can minimize this by doing batch-baking of your favorite artisan bread recipes. You can freeze the loaves and to make it even more time saving, you can slice up the loaves and wrap them up in portions and simply grab a portion out the freezer whenever you need bread.

Chapter 1

Must-Have Equipment and Utensils

---◆◆◆---

When you are ready to start baking artisan bread you will need several utensils and some kitchen equipment. Most people have the majority of these items in their kitchen. It is however good to go over the list of everything you must have to make baking fun instead of frustrating. As with any list of equipment, there will be some that you can use an alternative for if you do not have that specific item. Remember there will always be non-essentials that are great to have, but you can consider getting these at a later stage after you have all the essentials in place.

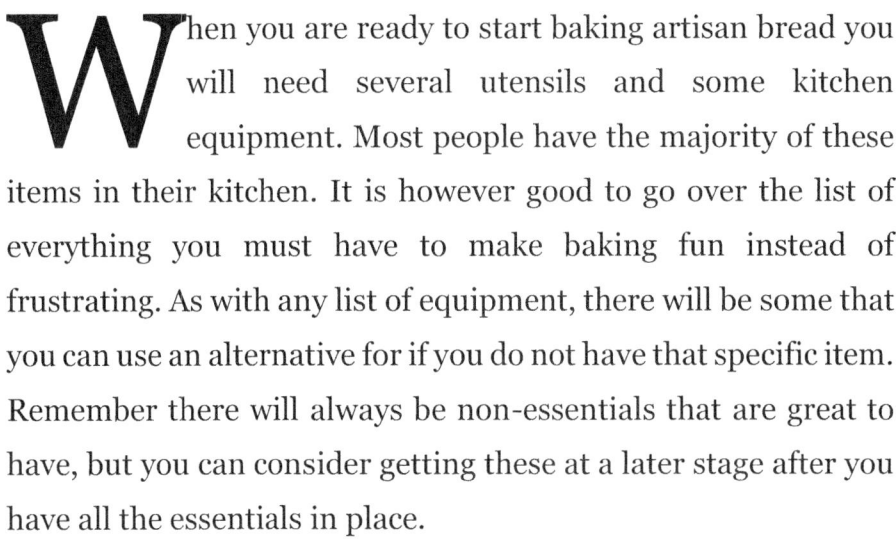

Assortment of Knives

For baking, you basically need two knives: a serrated edge knife and a chef's knife. You can multitask with these two knives for whatever tasks during the baking process.

Baking Pans (Various)

You need a good selection of baking pans to enable you to make different styles of artisan bread. The following are the most used baking pans you should invest in:

- Muffin pan
- Loaf pan
- Baking sheet
- Square pan
- Rectangular pan
- Round cake pan

Bowls for Mixing

Mixing bowls are made from different materials with stainless steel, glass, plastic, and ceramic being used the most. It is always a personal choice which materials you prefer. Keep in mind though that stainless steel and plastic are lightweight materials and cannot break, giving the best service. To start baking you need two large and two medium-sized mixing bowls.

Cooling Wire Rack

A wire cooling rack is an essential item for any baker. You need to have air circulate underneath your bread while it cools down. Placing your bread on a solid surface is not an option as you will have a soggy bottom crust that ruins your bread.

Digital Kitchen Scale

It is mentioned throughout this book that measuring ingredients precisely is always recommended to ensure successful baking. A good digital kitchen scale is a kitchen essential for any household and a good investment.

Food Processor or Stand Mixer

Here again, it comes down to personal preference as to whether you want to use a stand mixer or a food processor for making bread. A stand mixer with a dough hook will take a lot of the heavy work from you to get your bread dough kneaded and ready.

Should you want a true workhorse when it comes to kneading dough, invest in a food processor. It is powerful enough to easily knead almost every kind of dough and the blades will work your dough into elasticity within a few minutes.

Kitchen Towels (Cotton)

You always need kitchen towels for baking. Make sure that you have good quality cotton kitchen clothes on hand. It is not a good idea to use terry cloth kitchen towels for baking as they give off lint.

Kitchen Towels (Paper)

Paper towels are biodegradable and one of the best kitchen helpers available. Always keep a roll on hand when baking to help with cleaning and mopping up spills.

Lame and Docker

Many bread recipes will state that you need a lame or a docker to score your loaves of bread before baking. These are non-essential tools and you can use a good knife, a razor blade, or a box cutter instead. These alternatives work equally well for scoring.

Measuring Spoons and Cups

You need a set of measuring spoons consisting of six spoons to give you the biggest range of measurements. For measuring cups, you need two sets, one set for liquid and one set to measure dry ingredients. The reason you need a separate set of spoons to measure liquid is that these spoons are specifically measured with an extra space at the top that aids in preventing spills. Measuring cups for dry ingredients have a straight edge to enable you to easily level off the ingredients being measured.

Nonstick Cooking Spray

This is a kitchen essential as it is much easier to use than butter or oil for baking. There are several types available and it is a personal preference as to what you find is best suited to your needs. The best options are as follows:

- Avocado oil spray
- Canola oil spray
- Olive oil spray
- A blend of vegetable oils spray

Ovens

For baking artisan bread there are three options. You can use the oven in a standard stove, as well as invest in a good quality Dutch oven. A third option is a bread-making machine, but this is a non-essential luxury. Investing in a Dutch oven gives you so much more. These cast iron pots can be used for just about anything on a stovetop as well as inside a standard oven.

If you don't have a Dutch oven and you want to make a recipe specifying the use of one, you can successfully use any casserole dish with a lid, or a clay pot, or an oven-safe cooking pot. To ensure a good fit for the lid, place parchment paper over the pot or dish that you use and then put the lid on.

Parchment Paper

Parchment paper is the absolute go-to for bakers. It makes removing bread from the baking pans easy and you never have to battle with bread that stubbornly sticks in the pans. When baking in a Dutch oven you simply line the inside of the pot with parchment paper and this forms a basket for the bread. After baking you simply lift out the bread by holding onto the edges of the paper.

Pastry Brush

Pastry brushes are inexpensive, so it is advised to always keep a few on hand for brushing egg wash, or milk, or butter over your bread and rolls before baking.

Pastry Blade

A pastry blade is also called a bencher or a bench blade. This is a stainless steel rectangular blade with a wood or plastic handle. This is the best tool to use when dividing bread dough and excellent for scraping clean any work surface in the kitchen.

Pastry Scraper

This is an inexpensive tool made from flexible plastic and has a flat and a curved end. It is great to lift the dough from surfaces without the dough tearing or separating and once you have a pastry scraper you will use it continuously for a multitude of tasks in the kitchen.

Plastic Wrap

Keeping a roll of plastic wrap is a must in every kitchen. In baking, it is a huge help to cover dough without the risk of dough sticking to cloth kitchen towels. Plastic wrap also prevents spillage when you have a very soft dough rising whereas paper towels or cloth kitchen towels are unable to prevent these mishaps.

Proofing Basket

A proofing basket is not essential when you start your journey of bread baking. Yes, it is a great item to have, so put it on your wish list for later. Starting out you can use any mixing bowl that is large enough to hold your dough without it rising over the top and spilling out.

Frying Pan/Saucepan

A medium-sized frying pan or saucepan is needed for any of the savory bread recipes that require you to sauté any ingredients.

Kitchen Shears

Good quality kitchen shears are an all-round kitchen helper not only for baking but for any snipping and cutting in the kitchen and work great for scoring bread as well instead of buying a lame.

Scrapers and Spatulas

You need to invest in at least two scrapers and two spatulas for your kitchen. The best choices here are silicone and rubber with silicone being the top choice as it can withstand much higher temperatures than rubber is able to.

Spoons (Wooden)

Long-handled wooden spoons are ancient and most likely a utensil used in prehistoric times. Make sure you have a selection of sturdy wooden spoons available so that you can quickly change between mixing bowls without having to wash the wooden spoon every time.

Thermometer

The most accurate way possible to measure temperatures is to use an instant-read thermometer. You can manually check whether a loaf is done by knocking on the bottom, but many recipes call for the use of an instant-read thermometer to read internal temperatures of the bread that you are baking. So, it is always a good investment to get one.

Timer

A timer is essential when you bake bread to prevent overcooked disasters that nobody really wants to eat. Not all stoves have a built-in timer and this can cause problems. A timer is an inexpensive item that can save you a lot of frustration and a good kitchen gadget to have on hand.

Whisk

It is advisable to have at least two whisks in different sizes. The top choices are metal and silicone whisks, so make sure you have those on hand in your kitchen.

Chapter 2

Steps in Bread Making

These steps in bread making are your guideline through the bread making process. Please note that not all recipes will require each of the steps and not all the checks will be done for all recipes. This is your personal checklist to help you along especially as you begin your journey into bread making to help you to not skip steps, and also to help you check that you have done everything in order. This checklist is extremely handy when you start trying out new recipes to prevent mistakes and achieve success every time.

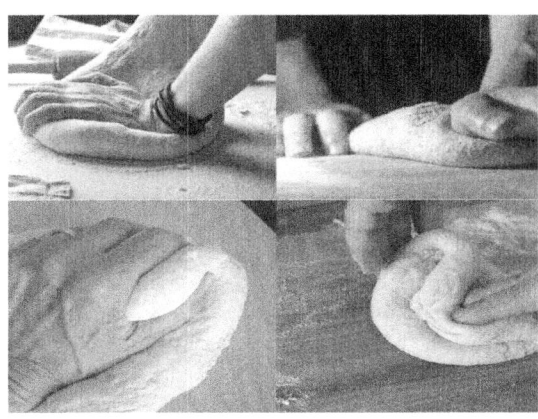

Step 1: Preparation

Prepping is the most important part of baking. First of all, place all your ingredients out on your kitchen table or counter and count them to make sure everything is there. Then place all the utensils, appliances, and equipment needed for the specific recipe out as well.

Step 2: Weigh and Measure Ingredients

It may sound like a lot of extra work but when you weigh and measure your ingredients out, place each into a separate bowl or container. This is a way to check that you have not missed or skipped any ingredients. Make doing this a habit right from the start of your baking journey.

Step 3: Knead, Mix, and Combine

Follow the recipe strictly and place the ingredients into the mixing bowl in the order the recipe tells you to do so. If you use yeast that needs to rest, follow the instructions and rest it for the specified time. Then add the rest of the ingredients to the mixing bowl.

Next, you will mix with a wooden spoon, or combine the ingredients in a food processor or stand mixer. If your recipe is for a no-knead bread this is the end of Step 3. If your recipe requires kneading you will now knead the dough by hand on a well-floured surface, or in a mixer, or food processor.

Step 4: First Rising (Resting Period)

This is the first resting period to allow the dough to rise until doubled in size. You cannot skip this step and if you do, your bread will be flat and inedible. When the dough rises it aerates the bread and makes it light and fluffy. Place the dough into a greased or floured bowl, cover it with cling wrap and a clean kitchen cloth, and do not disturb it until it has doubled in size.

Step 5: Stretch, Fold, Punch Down, and Shape

How this step progresses depends on the type of bread you are making and the specific recipe. After the first rising you rework the dough in one of the following ways.

- Kneaded bread: You punch the dough down.
- If the recipe requires, you will stretch the dough to improve the elasticity and do extra kneading of the dough.
- Next, you will shape the dough and put it into a prepared loaf pan, or a baking sheet. If using a Dutch oven, you will place the shaped bread directly into the Dutch oven for the second rising.
- You can also use a proofing basket and place the dough into the basket for the second resting period.

Step 6: Second Rising (Resting Period)

The second rest period is to further aerate the dough and improve the airy texture. You again allow the dough to rise until it has doubled in size.

Step 7: First Check

To check if the dough has risen sufficiently, pinch off a small piece and drop it into a glass of water. Dough that has formed enough air bubbles will rise to the top. This tells you that you can now continue with the next step in the baking process. If the dough sinks downwards you need to allow for extra rising time. Check the dough in 30-minute periods and do the glass and dough test every 30 minutes until the dough rises to the surface.

Step 8: Preheat

Roughly 30 minutes before the end of the second rising period you switch on your oven to preheat it to the required temperature. It is important that your oven is ready when the bread has sufficiently risen otherwise your dough will over-rise if you have to wait for the oven to reach the correct temperature.

Step 9: Second Check

When the dough is ready to go into the oven you perform the second check. Gently press into the dough with a finger. The dough is ready when it feels like you are pressing into a marshmallow. Remember that bread making has a margin for change, and your dough might need extra rising. There is nothing wrong if it needs this, it is normal.

Step 10: Bake

Always insert your oven rack in the center and place the baking pan on the rack. If you use a Dutch oven, place the Dutch oven, with the lid on, on the center rack for the required baking time as per your recipe.

To test whether the bread is baked through, remove bread from the baking pan and knock on the bottom of the loaf with your knuckles. If you hear a hollow sound, the bread is baked. If you don't hear the hollow sound, return the bread to the oven and continue baking, testing every 10 minutes.

Step 11: Third Check (for Dutch Ovens Only)

Halfway through the specified baking time, open the Dutch oven by removing the lid. Continue baking without the lid to allow the bread to form a crust.

Step 12: Cool Down

This is the final step in the baking process. Remove the bread from the baking pan and place it on a wire cooling rack. Do not allow the bread to cool down in the baking pan, as it will make bottom and side crusts soggy.

Chapter 3

Bread Baking Terms Explained

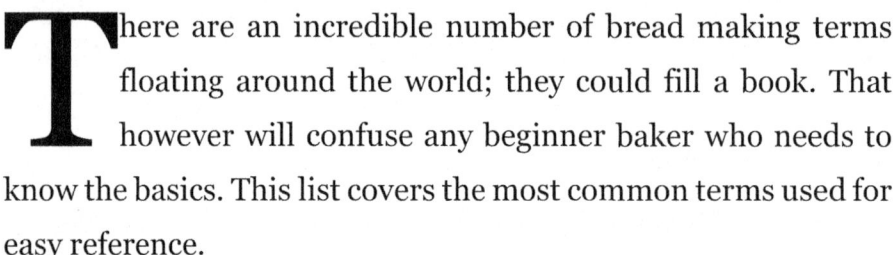

There are an incredible number of bread making terms floating around the world; they could fill a book. That however will confuse any beginner baker who needs to know the basics. This list covers the most common terms used for easy reference.

Autolyze

The process of mixing flour and water, then setting it aside to rest to promote the better formation of gluten.

Baguette

This refers to any long, cylindrical-shaped bread.

Banneton

This is a proofing basket where you put the dough to rest and rise and these baskets are usually made from wood, bamboo, or plastic.

Batard

Batard refers to any loaf of bread with a torpedo shape in all different types of cuisine.

Benching/Scaling

This is the step that follows after fermentation. You divide your dough into however many loaves you are making, shape them and place them into the loaf baking pans. Then you let them rest for a specific period of time.

Biga/Poolish/Sponge

These terms refer to pre-ferments that are usually made with commercial yeast and then added to the bread dough for better rising and improved flavor.

Boule

Boule refers to all loaves that are round whether they are free shaped or formed in a banneton.

Caramelization

Caramelization happens when sugar reaches 325 degrees F (162 degrees C) and when caramelization happens the bread develops a rich brown crust.

Cloche

This is a ceramic bowl with a lid that imitates the baking action of a steam-injected oven.

Couche

A piece of unbleached and untreated flax linen used to support bread dough such as baguettes during the proofing stage.

Crumb

This refers to the soft interior of a loaf of bread, as well as to the pattern of holes found inside the bread.

Degassing

This refers to what you do when you punch down the dough, you literally expel the carbon dioxide from the dough. Degassing also has an effect on the size of the holes that will form in the dough during the final rising period.

Direct Method and Indirect Method

When a recipe tells you to use the direct method to combine ingredients it means you simply add all the ingredients at once and then mix until the dough forms. This method is often referred to as making straight dough, without using a pre-ferment.

The indirect method is when you make the dough in separate stages, such as using a pre-ferment and then creating (building) the dough after the pre-fermentation process has been completed.

Dough: Lean, Enriched, and Rich

Bread dough is classified as follows:

- The dough is lean dough when no enriching products such as fat or sugar etc. are added.

- The dough is enriched dough when sugar, dairy, eggs, or fats are added to the dough.
- It is called rich dough when enrichment products are heavily added in far greater quantities than for enriched dough.

Elasticity

This is the ability of the dough to be stretched and formed into shapes.

Fermentation

This is the process when yeast breaks down sugar into carbon dioxide gas and alcohol. Fermentation gas is then trapped by the gluten in the dough. The gas trapped by the gluten expands and the dough rises.

Folding Ingredients in

This is when you gently combine ingredients and refrain from stirring or beating the ingredients. Most often this refers to combining ingredients that have previously been whipped or beaten into a dough or batter.

Hydration

Hydration is when liquid, mostly in the form of water, is absorbed by the other ingredients in the dough. Yeast must hydrate for fermentation to start and flour must hydrate for gluten to bond in the dough.

Kneading

Kneading is done when you work the dough either by hand—using the heel of your hand—or by using a stand mixer, or a food processor with a dough hook attachment. Kneading strengthens the strands of gluten and the dough develops into a pliant, soft mass.

Mixing

This is combing the ingredients for the dough by hand with a spoon, or using a food processor, or stand mixer to do the same.

Mother Starter

This is a starter created from wild yeast that you keep alive by feeding it regularly with water and flour. A mother starter can keep indefinitely in the fridge. You can then create other starters from the mother starter and bake with the new starters while keeping your mother starter going.

Oven Spring

We have referred to the oven spring in Chapter 4 under common mistakes. Bread dough rises quite a lot during the initial 10 minutes of baking and increases in volume between 10-15% and this rising time is called oven spring.

Proofing

Proofing has two meanings in bread making. It can refer to the process where you proof yeast to activate it, and it can refer to the final rising time before baking.

Punching Down

This is kneading the dough for a short while to release gas so that the dough can be ready for a second rising stage, this process is often referred to as degassing the dough.

Retard

This is slowing down the process of fermentation and allows you to place the dough in a tightly covered container in the refrigerator to continue with the baking process the next day or a few days later. Always cover the dough when you retard so that the dough does not dry out.

Scoring

Scoring the dough is when you cut slashes across the top of the loaf to create air vents for the gasses to escape during baking.

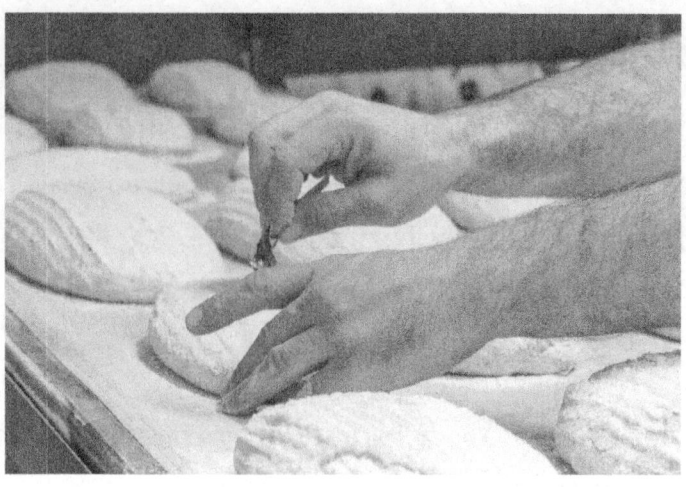

Soaker

This is a pre-dough containing one or more grains, salt, and water which is non-fermented. The pre-dough is made to start the enzyme activity before the dough is fermented.

Sourdough

This refers to any type of bread that is made from wild yeast.

Starter

A starter can be a pre-ferment made from commercial yeast or from wild yeast. A starter is used as leavening to make the bread dough rise.

Windowpane Test

This is the test done to determine if the gluten in the dough has developed sufficiently. If you can stretch the dough gently between your fingers and it does not break apart but forms a translucent 'window' the gluten is developed sufficiently for you to continue the bread-making process.

Chapter 4

Common Mistakes

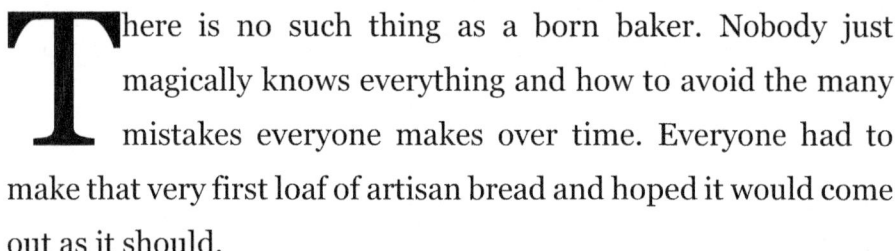

There is no such thing as a born baker. Nobody just magically knows everything and how to avoid the many mistakes everyone makes over time. Everyone had to make that very first loaf of artisan bread and hoped it would come out as it should.

The most important lesson for every beginner baker is to accept that things do not always turn out as they should, that it is not the end of the world, and that every failure someone else has made is helping you to avoid them.

Adding Salt to Yeast

You cannot add salt directly on top of yeast in your mixing bowl. This is the fastest way to kill yeast and you will be left with a loaf of bread that sadly resembles a frisbee. The solution is very simple. Add the yeast and salt on opposite sides of the mixing bowl and swirl the salt around with a spoon to mix it with the flour. Another option is to add the salt to the measured flour and mix it in before adding the flour to the mixing bowl.

Bottom Is Burnt

If the bottom crust of the bread is burnt when the bread is not completely baked yet, it means your oven rack is too close to the element in the oven. The optimal position for the oven rack is in the center slot in the oven and ensures even baking.

Browns Too Fast

It can happen that the bread browns faster than it should. To prevent the bread from burning before it is thoroughly baked through, simply make a small tent from aluminum foil and place it over the bread in the oven as a heat shield. It is important to not take the bread out of the oven before the cooking time stated in the recipe. Undercooked bread is not pleasant tasting at all.

Dense Bread

When your bread comes out as a rather flat, dense loaf it is normally due to one of two reasons.

- Your yeast came into direct contact with the salt you added, as discussed higher up as a mistake bakers make.
- The yeast used is past its expiry date. It is important not to stockpile yeast, but instead, buy fresh when you want to bake. Always discard yeast past its sell-by date.

Dough Too Dry

The texture of the dough differs from recipe to recipe. One recipe will have a wet, sticky dough while another recipe will have a stiff, much drier dough. Both are correct for their specific recipes. Unfortunately, many novice bakers feel that the wet, sticky dough should not be like that and they then add extra flour to the dough to make it less sticky. Always follow the recipe exactly and should the dough be too wet, make notes and then adjust the flour the next time you use this specific recipe. Never just add extra liquid because you think it feels or looks too dry or add flour because the dough is sticky and wet.

Heat Escapes During Baking

The first 20 minutes of baking is called "oven spring" and a very important part of the bread rising. If you open the oven door during the first 20 minutes, you will lose the rising that should happen, and you will also have a soft crust instead of a good crunchy crust.

Know Your Yeast

Yeast can be tricky and confusing to use as we are confronted with so many different types of yeast. It is not surprising that beginner bakers can find this off-putting and it stops them from trying new recipes. When you are confused about which yeast to use, refer to this breakdown to guide you to the correct one to use in a specific recipe. Some yeasts are interchangeable in recipes, but results may differ slightly.

Cake Yeast

Cake yeast (also called compressed yeast) is small blocks of live yeast, fresh and moist. This is the traditional yeast used for generations and today only really used by some professional bakers as the modern yeasts available are easier to use. This yeast is extremely perishable and must be refrigerated or frozen.

Active Dry Yeast

This is the most commonly used form of yeast used and is available in shops everywhere. This yeast comes in small ¼-oz sealed packets and needs to be proofed before being added to the flour.

Instant Yeast

Instant yeast is known by many different names such as fast-rising yeast, or quick rise yeast. What makes this type of yeast different is that it does not need proofing and is added dry directly into the mixing bowl holding the flour. The instant yeast granules are smaller than the granules of active dry yeast.

Bread Machine Yeast

Bread machine yeast is instant yeast, simply called by another name, and comes in different packaging and often contains ascorbic acid as a dough conditioner.

Rapid Rise Yeast

Rapid rise yeast does not have to be proofed and is added directly to the flour. Rapid rise yeast is instant yeast with an added dough conditioner in the form of ascorbic acid.

Wild Yeast (Sourdough Starter)

Sourdough bread uses a very different type of yeast than other types of bread. For this, you either need to grow your own yeast starter or buy your sourdough starter kit commercially.

Measure and Weigh

The majority of recipes around today give the measures of ingredients in cups. That is all good, but it is not the most accurate way to measure bread ingredients. Cups often differ and this can cause your dough to be off, and your bread to not turn out as perfectly as you want it to be. It is one of the absolute must-haves for any kitchen and baking to invest in a good scale. Look at the online outlets and compare different kitchen scales and prices to get the very best to suit your specific needs and your budget.

Not Keeping Dough Covered

When the dough rises it does not want to be exposed to air. What happens is that a skin forms over the top of the dough and this prevents the dough from rising sufficiently. Make it a habit from day one to never leave your dough uncovered. Cover the bowl with cling wrap and then throw a clean cloth over that to keep your dough away from air. Do this even if you are in the middle of mixing and you need to leave for a few minutes to attend to something else.

Notes

Taking notes is not old fashioned; professional bakers always jot down notes. This is to help you in the future, it is a way for you to learn aspects about a specific recipe to improve on it. For instance, the bread is too crumbly, or you prefer a less dense texture. Making notes means you can make adjustments safely the next time you use this recipe. You can make notes about adding more or less salt, or what other condiments you find work great with any savory loaf.

Scoring

When we see photos of different artisan loaves it is always noticeable that they have pretty and often very decorative scoring in the top crust. Yes, some bakers get quite inventive with the scoring patterns they make, but it really is not about the pretty and decorative factor at all. If you do not score the bread, it will rise unevenly and may crack open on the sides. The bread needs air vents and that is what scoring does and the bread is thus able to rise completely as it should.

Steam in the Oven

Steam is important in the baking process if you want a good crust on the bread. There are two ways in which to easily create steam in your oven at home. You can use whichever method works best for you personally.

- Place a shallow ovenproof dish filled halfway with warm water on the bottom rack of your oven and leave it there for the first 20-25 minutes of the baking time. Then remove the dish or pan and allow the bread to bake for the rest of the stipulated time.

- You can fill a spray bottle with water and immediately after placing the bread in the oven, spray the interior of the oven as well as your loaf of bread with the water and close the oven quickly to trap the steam inside.

Switching Flour

Recipes are created using specific types of flour and all the ingredients are based on that specific flour. Usually, recipes will tell you if you can use another type of flour and what flour is compatible with that recipe. To swap out flour willy nilly if you prefer another type is a recipe for disaster with flat, dense bread that does not taste good at all. The best thing to do if you prefer to use a specific type of flour is to find a recipe created using that flour.

Temperatures

Temperature plays a critical role in the success of bread baking. Professional bakers have written books on the temperatures to use and often they simply confuse novice bakers instead of enlightening them.

Follow these simple rules regarding temperatures and you will achieve success with baking artisan bread:

- Always follow the instructions in any specific recipe. They tell you the perfect temperature to bake at, and whether you should use warm or cold liquids etcetera.
- Always follow the baking temperature and time given in a recipe. The temperature and time have been calculated for the optimal baking time at the exact temperature to ensure the best results.
- In general, using boiling water is a huge no-no. You kill the yeast and your bread will flop. When a recipe states use warm or hot water this means 100-130 degrees F (37-54 degrees C).
- High altitude baking: Your baking is definitely affected when you live at very high altitudes and you must make adjustments for this. This can be difficult, but not impossible to do, you must experiment and find what baking temperatures, baking times, and what ingredient

adjustments work best for you. Two things to try is to lower the oven temperature and to reduce the amount of yeast you use by ¼. Take notes and you will soon be able to juggle things and bake great bread.

Too Impatient to Wait

It is quite understandable that bakers get impatient and that they want to get the bread in and out of the oven in the fastest possible time. Unfortunately, bread does not work that way, not bread using yeast that is. Proofing the dough is a critical step in baking fluffy, delicious bread. A tip when looking at recipes is that if the rising time is too long to suit you, it is better to look for another recipe with a much shorter rising time. It is not worth the effort to under-proof dough and end up with a flop.

The way to test whether your bread has proofed enough is to push your finger gently into the dough. If the dough springs back quickly and the indentation where you pushed your finger into the dough disappears very fast, you need to let the dough proof some more. You can keep testing every 10-15 minutes and when the indentation of your finger takes a long time to disappear, your dough is adequately proofed.

Too Much Liquid

The liquid can make or break your loaf of bread. The rule you should always follow is that although the recipe gives you a specific measure of liquid to add, do not add it all at once. Start off slowly and remember you can always add more, but once you have added the liquid you cannot remove it again. So, add just enough liquid to enable you to form a ball of dough and to be able to clean it from the bottom of the mixing bowl. Keep adding small amounts of liquid until you see your dough come together and then stop. Sometimes you may even have to add more liquid than stated in the recipe, this is not unusual in baking.

Chapter 5

Easy, Basic Bread

Starting out baking artisan bread at home can be intimidating for beginners. To make it easy to start baking, we have a few simple and easy to make loaves to try and master.

Sandwich Loaf

This is the classic loaf to use for all types of sandwiches, to make toasted sandwiches, and French toast. It slices easily and has a golden crust with a soft interior.

Time: 2 hours 42 minutes

Serving Size: 1 slice (16 servings), makes 1 loaf

Prep Time: 12 minutes (plus 2 hours rising time)

Cook Time: 30 to 40 minutes

Nutritional Facts/Info:

Calories 120

Carbs 19 g

Fat 3 g

Protein 3 g

Ingredients

3 cups	13.2 oz	361 g	All-purpose flour
½-⅔ cup	41.1-5.5 oz	113-152 g	Hot water, enough to make a smooth, soft dough
½ cup	4 oz	113 g	Milk, lukewarm, with a fat content of own choice
4 tbsp	2 oz	56 g	Butter melted or
¼ cup	1.7 oz	50 g	Vegetable oil of personal preference
2 tbsp	9.1 oz	4	Sugar, granulated
2 ¼ tsp	¼ oz	7 g	Active dry yeast dissolved in 1 tbsp of warm water or instant yeast without the added water
1 ¼ tsp	0.3 oz	7.5 g	Salt

Directions

1. Combine all the ingredients in a large mixing bowl and stir with a wooden spoon until a soft dough comes together that pulls away from the sides of the bowl.

2. Lightly grease a work surface and turn the dough out onto this surface.

3. Oil your hands and knead the dough for roughly 6-8 minutes until the dough is supple and smooth. Alternatively use a stand mixer or a food processor with a dough hook to mix the dough until smooth.

4. Grease a bowl and transfer the dough to this bowl. Cover with plastic wrap or a kitchen towel and leave the dough to rise for 1-2 hours until the dough has risen to nearly double in size. The temperature in the kitchen will determine the rising time.

5. Gently punch down the dough and turn it out onto a greased surface. Roll the dough into an oblong shape and then transfer the dough to a greased loaf pan (8 ½ x 4 ½ x 2 ½ inches) (21 x 11 x 6 cm)

6. Cover the pan with oiled plastic wrap and leave to rise for 1 hour. The dough should be risen with a domed shape and protrude above the pan roughly 1 inch. Test the readiness of the dough by pressing your finger into the side. If it rebounds slowly, the dough is ready.

7. Roughly 30 minutes before the end of the second rising, switch on the oven to preheat to 350 degrees F (175 degrees C).

8. Bake the bread until it is a light golden brown, for about 30-35 minutes. Do the test to see if it is done by rapping

your knuckles on the bottom. If the sound is hollow, the bread is done.

9. Remove the bread from the baking pan and leave to cool down on a cooling rack before slicing. Bread can be stored at room temperature in a plastic bag.

Milk Bread

This is a soft milk bread in the Japanese style, much like brioche, but does not have the strong egg taste of brioche.

Time: 2 hours 5 minutes

Serving Size: 1 slice (8 servings), makes 1 loaf

Prep Time: 15 minutes (plus 1 hour 30 minutes rising time)

Cook Time: 20 minutes

Nutritional Facts/Info:

Calories 196.4

Carbs 26.7 mg

Fat 7.4 mg

Protein 5.6 mg

Ingredients

1 ¾ cups plus 1 tbsp	7 ⅓ oz plus 0.27 oz	210 g plus 7.5 g	Bread flour
¾ tsp	0.15 oz	4.5 g	Salt
2 tbsp	0.9 oz	24 g	White sugar
1 ½			Eggs
2 ¼ tsp	¼ oz	7 g	Active dry yeast
¼ cup plus 1 tbsp	2 oz plus 0.5 oz	59 g plus 14 g	Milk
¾ cup	6 oz	177 g	Water warm
¼ cup	2 oz	57 g	Butter cubed

Directions

1. Place the sugar, bread flour, yeast, and salt into the bowl of a stand mixer or a food processor and combine on low speed using the dough hook. Add the eggs to the mixture and incorporate.

2. Mix in the milk and the warm water and lastly add the butter. Combine until everything is fully incorporated.

3. Continue mixing until a dough forms that holds together. When the dough becomes translucent the mixing is complete. Should you have difficulty getting the dough to be translucent, add small amounts of flour or milk until this consistency is reached.

4. Set dough aside to rise until it has doubled in size.

5. Shape the dough into an oblong and place in a greased loaf pan (9 x 5 ½ x 3 inches) (23 x 13 x 7 cm).

6. Allow the dough to rise for 30-60 minutes again until it reaches about 1 inch (2.5 cm) below the rim of the pan.

7. About 30 minutes into the second rising, switch on the oven and preheat to 350 degrees F (175 degrees C).

8. Cut a 2-inch slit lengthwise into the top of the bread with a sharp knife or scissors.

9. Bake the bread for roughly 20 minutes and test with a thermometer for doneness. The internal temperature should be 200 degrees F (93 degrees C).

10. Turn out onto a wire cooling rack and allow to cool down completely before slicing.

Rustic Bread

This is a very easy recipe for a basic rustic artisan loaf, with no intricate steps to follow, and only 5 ingredients.

Time: 6 hours 15 minutes

Serving Size: 1 slice (10 servings) makes 1 loaf

Prep Time: 15 minutes (plus 5 hours 40 minutes rising time)

Cook Time: 20 minutes

Nutritional Facts/Info:

Calories 161

Carbs 33.7 g

Fat 0.5 g

Protein 4.8 g

Ingredients

1 ½ cups	12 oz	345 g	Water, warm
¼ cup	1 ¼ oz	34.5 g	Cornmeal
3 ¼ cups	12 ¾ oz	390 g	All-purpose flour
2 ¼ tsp	0.45 oz	13.5 g	Salt, coarse
2 ¼ tsp	¼ oz	7 g	Active dry yeast

Directions

1. Put the water and salt into a large bowl and stir to dissolve the salt. Then add the yeast and stir for about 10 minutes until the mixture is foamy.

2. Add the flour to the yeast mixture and stir until everything is well combined. This will be a very wet looking and loose dough, that is normal. Cover the bowl with oiled plastic wrap or a damp kitchen cloth and set aside for roughly 5 hours.

3. Dust a working surface with cornmeal. Then shape the dough into a round ball with wet hands and place on the cornmeal covered surface. Score the top of the bread with

several cuts with a sharp knife. Let the bread rest for 30-60 minutes until it has doubled in size.

4. Preheat the oven to 425 degrees F (220 degrees).

5. Place the dough on a greased baking sheet and place it on the center slot in the oven.

6. Spray the surface of the bread a few times with water during the 20-minute baking time. The bread is done when it is golden brown.

Soda Bread with Cheese and Onion

This is easy to make soda bread that does not need yeast with the great taste of onion and cheddar.

Time: 55 minutes

Serving Size: 1 slice (6 servings), makes 1 loaf

Prep Time: 15 minutes (plus 10 minutes cooling time)

Cook Time: 30 minutes

Nutritional Facts/Info:

Calories 264 calories

Carbs 23.7 mg

Fat 9.1 g

Protein 8.2 g

Ingredients

2 cups	8 ⅔ oz	240 g	Bread flour
1 ½ tsp	0.15 oz	6 g	Baking powder
½ cup plus 2 tbsp	4 oz plus 1 oz	118 g plus 28 g	Buttermilk
¼ cup plus 2 tbsp	1 ¼ oz plus 0.64 oz	38 g plus 9.4 g	Onion, finely chopped
¾ tsp	3 1/16 oz	4.5 g	Salt
3 tbsp	1.5 oz	42 g	Butter, softened
1 tbsp plus ¼ tsp	0.3 oz plus 0.025 oz	7.5 g plus 0.625 g	Confectioners' sugar (powdered sugar)
¼ cup plus 1 tbsp	1 oz plus 0.25 oz	29 g plus 7 g	Cheddar cheese, shredded

Instructions

1. Preheat the oven to 425 degrees F (220 degrees C) and prepare a baking sheet by placing a sheet of parchment paper into the baking sheet.
2. Place the bread flour, baking powder, and salt into a large mixing bowl and whisk to combine.
3. Add the softened butter, confectioners' sugar, and the buttermilk into the mixing bowl and mix thoroughly until you have a soft dough.
4. Add the shredded cheese and the chopped onion and gently fold into the dough mixture.
5. Shape the dough into a round ball and place it on the prepared baking sheet. Gently flatten the ball of dough to a 2-inch thickness and dust the dough with flour.
6. Place into the oven and bake for roughly 30 minutes, until the bread is browned.
7. Place on a wire cooling rack for a few minutes and serve warm or lukewarm.

Dinner Rolls

These are classic yeast dinner rolls and taste best fresh on the day they are made.

Time: 1 hour 30 minutes

Serving Size: 1 roll, the recipe makes 12 rolls

Prep Time: 40 minutes (plus 30 minutes rising time)

Cook Time: 20 minutes

Nutritional Facts/Info:

Calories 106

Carbs 18.5 g

Fat 2.3 g

Protein 2.5 g

Ingredients

2 cups	9 oz	240 g	All-purpose flour
2 ¼ tsp	¼ oz	7 g	Rapid rise yeast
½ tsp	0.1 oz	3 g	Salt
2 tbsp	0.86 oz	24 g	Sugar
¼ cup	2 oz	59 g	Water
½ cup	4 oz	118 g	Milk
2 tbsp	1 oz	28 g	Butter or margarine

Instructions

1. Place ¾ cup (3 ¼ oz) (90 g) of flour into the bowl of an electric stand mixer and add the salt, sugar, and dry yeast to the bowl. Make sure that you do not put the yeast and salt together.

2. Heat the water, butter, and milk until warm, 120-130 degrees F (48-54 degrees C).

3. Add the warm milk mixture to the flour mixture and beat on medium speed for 2 minutes. Scrape the bowl to make sure you incorporate everything.

4. Add ¼ cup (1 1/16 oz) (30 g) of flour to the mixture in the bowl and beat on high speed for 2 minutes.

5. Do not put the remainder of the flour in the bowl all at once. Stir in small quantities until you have a soft dough.

6. Place the dough on a floured surface and knead for about 8-10 minutes until the dough is elastic and smooth.

7. Cover the dough and leave it to rest for about 10 minutes.

8. Divide the dough into 12 equal portions and shape these into balls.

9. Grease an 8-inch round baking pan and place the rolls into the pan.

10. Cover the pan and leave it in a warm place in the kitchen to rise for about 30 minutes, until the rolls have tripled in size.

11. Preheat the oven to 375 degrees F (190 degrees C). Place the oven pan in the center of the oven and bake rolls for 20 minutes until they are brown and done.

12. Remove the rolls from the pan and brush them with melted butter (this is optional).

13. Serve the rolls warm.

Chapter 6

No-Knead Loaves

N o-knead bread and loaves are extremely popular as not everyone likes or has the time to knead dough, fold, punch down, and stretch the dough. It is always good to have a selection of no-knead bread recipes on hand for any baker, both novice and experienced.

Beer Bread with Honey and Oats

Beer bread is always popular, so this one has the added taste of honey and oats. It is quick and very easy to make.

Time: 35 minutes

Serving Size: 1 slice (12 servings), makes 1 loaf

Prep Time: 5 minutes

Cook Time: 30 minutes

Nutritional Facts/Info:

Calories 161.7

Carbs 25.7 g

Fat 4.6 g

Protein 3.4 g

Ingredients

2 cups	8 ½ oz	240 g	All-purpose flour
1 tbsp	0.1 oz	4 g	Baking powder
1 ¼ cup	4 ⅜ oz	124 g	Oats, rolled
1 tsp	0.15 oz	4.2 g	Brown sugar
1 tsp	0.2 oz	6 g	Salt
1 bottle	12 fluid oz	340 g (355 ml)	Beer
1 tbsp	¾ oz	21 g	Honey
¼ cup	2 oz	57 g	Butter, melted

Directions

1. Preheat the oven to 375 degrees F (190 degrees C) and grease a loaf pan (9 x 5 x 3 inches) (23 x 13 x 8 cm).
2. Place the oats, flour, salt, brown sugar, and baking powder into a large mixing bowl and stir to combine.
3. Trickle the honey over the ingredients in the mixing bowl and then pour the beer over all the ingredients. Mix to combine, but do not over mix.

4. Spoon the bread mixture into the greased loaf pan and then trickle the melted butter over the top of the bread.

5. Place in the oven and bake until the bread is golden brown, about 25-30 minutes. Test for doneness by inserting a knife into the bread. The bread is done when the knife comes out clean.

6. Place the loaf on a wire cooling rack before slicing.

Raisin Bread

This bread does not use yeast, so there is no rising time. Quick and easy to make, you can have this bread done within 1 hour.

Time: 1 hour 10 minutes

Serving Size: 1 slice (12 servings), makes 1 loaf

Prep Time: 10 minutes

Cook Time: 1 hour

Nutritional Facts/Info:

Calories 233

Carbs 43.2 g

Fat 5 g

Protein 4.8 g

Ingredients

½ cup	3 ½ oz	99 g	White sugar
3 cups	12 ¾ oz	360 g	All-purpose flour
½ tsp	0.05 oz	2 g	Baking soda
3 tsp	0.05 oz	2 g	Baking powder
¾ tsp	0.07 oz	2 g	Cinnamon, ground
1 tsp	0.2 oz	6 g	Salt
1			Egg
1 cup	5.3 oz	150 g	Raisins
1 cup	8 oz	227 g	Milk
¼ cup	2 oz	57 g	Butter, melted

Directions

1. Grease a 9 x 5 x 3 inches (23 x 13 x 8 cm) loaf pan and set aside.
2. Preheat the oven to 350 degrees F (175 degrees C).
3. Place the sugar, baking soda, flour, baking powder, cinnamon, salt, and raisins into a large mixing bowl and

stir well to combine, then make a well in the center of the bowl.

4. Put the egg into a small bowl and whisk until it is frothy. Then mix in the milk and the melted butter and pour this mixture into the well in the mixing bowl.

5. Stir the egg mixture into the dry ingredients using a wooden spoon until the ingredients are moistened. Do not over mix.

6. Spoon the bread mixture into the prepared loaf pan.

7. Place the bread into the oven and bake for 1 hour. Turn out onto a cooling rack to cool to room temperature before slicing.

8. Serve with butter.

Zucchini Bread

This bread is moist and will stay fresh in the fridge for a couple of weeks. It can also be frozen successfully

Time: 1 hour 40 minutes

Serving Size: 1 slice (12 servings), makes 1 loaf

Prep Time: 20 minutes (plus 20 minutes cool down in pan)

Cook Time: 1 hour

Nutritional Facts/Info:

Calories 225

Carbs 32.1 g

Fat 1.7 g

Protein 3.3 g

Ingredients

1 ½ cups	6 ⅜ oz	180 g	All-purpose flour
½ tsp	0.05 oz	2 g	Baking soda
½ tsp	0.1 oz	3 g	Salt
½ tsp	0.05 oz	2 g	Baking powder
1 1/2			Eggs
1 ½ tsp	0.14 oz	3.97 g	Cinnamon, ground
½ cup	3 ½ oz	99 g	Vegetable oil of own preference
1 ½ tsp	0.225 oz	6.3 g	Vanilla extract
1 cup plus 2 tbsp	7 oz plus 0.86 oz	99 g plus 24 g	White sugar
¾ cup	3.3 oz	94.5 g	Walnuts, chopped
3 cups	15.9 oz	450 g	Zucchini, grated

Directions

1. Preheat the oven to 325 degrees F (165 degrees C) and grease and flour one 9 x 5 x 3 inches (23 x 13 x 8 cm) loaf pan.

2. Sift the cinnamon, baking powder, salt, baking soda, and flour together into a large mixing bowl.

3. Place the sugar, egg, vanilla, and oil into a separate bowl and whisk.

4. Add the sifted dry ingredients to the egg mixture and beat to combine.

5. Stir the nuts and zucchini into the batter and combine well.

6. Pour the bread batter into the greased loaf pan.

7. Bake for about 40-60 minutes. Test by inserting a knife or tester into the bread and the bread is done when it comes out clean.

8. Remove bread from the oven and allow it to cool down for 20 minutes inside the baking pan.

9. Remove the bread from the baking pan and set it on a wire cooling rack to cool completely before serving.

Banana Loaf

This loaf is moist and can be served plain or with butter if preferred. It freezes well and if you slice the loaf before freezing, it is easy to take out a few slices at a time.

Time: 1 hour 35 minutes

Serving Size: 1 slice (12 servings), makes 1 loaf

Prep Time: 15 minutes

Cook Time: 1 hour 20 minutes

Nutritional Facts/Info:

Calories 306.8

Carbs 44.2 g

Fat 13.6 g

Protein 3.8 g

Ingredients

1 ¾ cups	7 ½ oz	210 g	All-purpose flour
1 cup	10.6 oz	300 g	Banana, mashed
2			Eggs, whisked
1 ½ cup	10 ½ oz	297 g	White sugar
⅓ cup	4 oz	118 g	Buttermilk
½ cup	2.2 oz	63 g	Pecans, chopped
½ cup	3 ½ oz	99 g	Vegetable oil of own choice
½ tsp	0.1 oz	3 g	Salt
1 tsp	0.1 oz	4 g	Baking soda

Directions

1. Spray a 9 x 5 x 3 inches (23 x 13 x 8 cm) loaf pan with vegetable oil and set aside.
2. Preheat the oven to 325 degrees F (154 degrees C).
3. Mix the mashed banana, oil, eggs, and buttermilk together in a large mixing bowl.
4. Sift the flour, salt, sugar, and baking soda together into a separate bowl.

5. Add the banana mixture to the sifted ingredients.

6. Add the chopped pecans to the mixing bowl and mix until all the ingredients are combined well.

7. Spoon the mixture into the prepared loaf pan and place the baking pan into the oven.

8. Bake the banana bread until a tester comes out clean, about 1 hour 20 minutes.

9. Place on a wire cooling rack to cool down and serve at room temperature.

Chapter 7

Kneaded Bread

Bread made by kneading the dough has been with us since ancient times. Today we have the option of kneading by hand or using a stand mixer or food processor equipped with dough hooks. Each step of the process must be followed to ensure great tasting bread with a crunchy crust and soft or chewy interiors, depending on the type of bread you choose.

Soda Bread

This is a basic Irish soda bread recipe with buttermilk added for enhanced flavor.

Time: 1 hour 15 minutes

Serving Size: 1 slice (12 servings), makes 1 round loaf

Prep Time: 15 minutes

Cook Time: 1 hour

Nutritional Facts/Info:

Calories 193

Carbs 39.6 g

Fat 1.5 g

Protein 5.6 g

Ingredients

3 cups	12 ¾ oz	360 g	All-purpose flour
½ tsp	0.1 oz	3 g	Salt
2 tsp	0.2 oz	8 g	Baking powder
½ cup	4.06 oz	115 g	White vinegar
½ cup	2 ¾ oz	79,5 g	Raisins
1 ½ cups	12 oz	345 g	Buttermilk
1 tbsp	0.24 oz	6.81 g	Caraway seeds
2			Eggs

Directions

1. Grease a springform baking pan and set aside.
2. Preheat the oven to 350 degrees F (175 degrees C).
3. Put the flour, salt, sugar, and baking powder into a large mixing bowl.
4. In a separate bowl whisk the eggs and the buttermilk and add the egg mixture to the bowl with the dry ingredients.
5. Lastly, add the raisins and stir the dough mixture to combine all the ingredients well.

6. Scrape the dough onto a lightly floured work surface and shape the dough into a round loaf. If the dough is very wet, add small amounts of extra flour until the dough no longer sticks to your fingers.

7. Place the dough ball into the prepared springform pan and sprinkle the caraway seeds over top.

8. Place the baking pan into the preheated oven and bake until the loaf is brown, about 1 hour.

9. Test for doneness by knocking on the bottom of the bread, if it sounds hollow the bread is done.

10. Place bread on a cooling rack and allow it to cool down before slicing.

Copycat Subway Buns

These copycat buns come out exactly like the famous Subway buns. Soft and delicious and perfect for making at home, they are a hit with everyone.

Time: 2 hours 15 minutes

Serving Size: ½ bun (8 servings), makes 4 9-inch subs

Prep Time: 15 minutes plus 1 hour 30 minutes rising time

Cook Time: 25 minutes

Nutritional Facts/Info:

Calories 244

Carbs 38.3 g

Fat 7.6 g

Protein 5.8 g

Ingredients

1 cup	8 oz	227 g	Water (110 degrees F, 43 degrees C)
4 tbsp (¼ cup)	1.88 oz	53.2 g	Oil olive
1 tbsp	0.43 oz	12 g	White sugar
2 ½ cups to 2 ¾ cups	10.6 oz to 11.6 oz	300 g to 330 g	All-purpose flour
1 tbsp	0.3 oz	8.5 g	Active dry yeast
1 ½ tsp	0.3 oz	9 g	Salt

Directions

1. Place the yeast, water, salt, olive oil, and sugar into the bowl of a stand mixer and stir. Let the mixture stand for about 5 minutes.
2. Add 1 cup of flour to the yeast mixture and mix for 3-5 minutes using the dough hook.
3. Add another cup of flour to the dough and again mix using the dough hook until the ingredients are combined.

4. Keep adding ¼ cup of flour at a time while mixing until you have a soft dough. Take note that the dough should still be sticky enough to stick to the bottom of the mixing bowl, but dry enough to start pulling away from the sides of the bowl.

5. When the dough has reached this stage, turn the dough ball out onto a lightly floured surface. Knead the dough until you have a very soft, smooth dough.

6. Return the dough ball to the mixing bowl and cover with oiled plastic wrap. Set aside for 30 minutes for the dough to rise.

7. Prepare a baking sheet by spraying it with vegetable oil or placing a sheet of parchment paper onto the baking sheet. You can also use a silicone baking mat inside the baking sheet.

8. Turn the dough out after 1 hour onto a lightly floured surface and divide it into four equal-sized pieces. Roll the four pieces out so that they resemble four very thin loaves measuring 9-10 inches (22.9 to 25.4 cm) long.

9. Place the four buns onto the prepared baking sheet. Please leave 2 inches of space between each bun.

10. Cover the buns with oiled plastic wrap and allow the dough to rise for 1 hour until the buns have doubled in size.

11. About 30 minutes into the rising, preheat the oven to 350 degrees F (175 degrees C).

12. Remove the plastic wrap and place the baking sheet into the oven and bake for 25 minutes.

13. Rub the tops of the buns with a stick of butter when they come out of the oven and then cover the buns with a kitchen dishcloth to cool down. Covering the buns with a cloth during the cooling down stage ensures that the buns stay soft.

14. Leave to cool down for 30 minutes before serving.

Italian Bread with Herbs

This recipe is very versatile as it is suitable for eating with a meal and can also be used as pizza dough.

Time: 2 hours 40 minutes

Serving Size: 1 slice (12 servings), makes 1 loaf

Prep Time: 30 minutes plus 1 hour 35 minutes rising time

Cook Time: 36 minutes

Nutritional Facts/Info:

Calories 37

Carbs 1.7 g

Fat 3 g

Protein 1.1 g

Ingredients

2 ½ cups plus 2 tbsp	10 ½ oz plus 0.54 oz	300 g plus 15 g	Bread flour
1 cup	8 oz	227 g	Water, warm (110 degrees F, 45 degrees C)
2 ¼ tsp	¼ oz	7 g	Yeast active dry
2 tbsp	0.939 oz	26.6 g	Olive oil
1 tbsp	0.43 oz	12 g	White sugar
1 ½ tsp	0.3 oz	9 g	Salt
1 ½ tsp	0.1 oz	1.52 g	Oregano
1 ½ tsp	0.04 oz	1.07 g	Dried basil
½ tsp	0.05 oz	1.17 g	Onion powder
½ tsp	0.058 oz	1.64 g	Garlic powder

¼ cup	1.06 oz	30 g	Romano cheese, grated

Directions

1. Place the warm water, yeast, and sugar into a large mixing bowl and stir to mix. Set aside until the mixture is foamy, about 5 minutes.

2. Stir the salt, onion powder, olive oil, garlic powder, herbs, cheese, and 1 cup of flour into the yeast mixture.

3. Add the rest of the flour gradually, mixing every time you add flour until you have a stiff dough.

4. Turn out the dough onto a floured work surface and knead until rubbery and smooth, for about 5-10 minutes.

5. Oil a bowl and place the dough ball inside. Turn the dough around so that the surface of the dough is coated with oil. Cover the dough with a damp kitchen cloth or greased plastic wrap and set aside until the dough has doubled in size, about 1 hour.

6. Prepare a 9 x 5 x 3 inches (23 x 13 x 8 cm) loaf pan by spraying it with vegetable oil. You can also use a baking sheet instead of a loaf pan.

7. Punch the dough down to release gas and air, and shape into an oblong loaf. Place the dough into the prepared loaf pan.

8. Set the pan aside and allow the dough to rise for another 30 minutes until it has again doubled in size.

9. At the beginning of the second rising phase, switch on the oven and preheat it to 350 degrees F (175 degrees C).

10. Place the loaf into the oven and bake until golden brown, for about 35 minutes.

11. Place baked bread on a cooling rack and allow to cool for a minimum of 15 minutes before slicing it.

Wheat and Honey Bread

A versatile bread that is suitable to be served with any meal.

Time: 2 hours

Serving Size: 1 slice (12 servings), makes 1 loaf

Prep Time: 30 minutes plus 1 hour for rising time

Cook Time: 30 minutes

Nutritional Facts/Info:

Calories 171.5

Carbs 31.2 g

Fat 3.5 g

Protein 4.3 g

Ingredients

1 cup	4.2 oz	120 g	Whole wheat flour
2 ½ cups	10.6 oz	300 g	All-purpose flour
1 cup	8 oz	227 g	Warm water (110 degrees F, 45 degrees C)
1 ½ tsp	0.16 oz	4.5 g	Active dry yeast
2 tbsp plus 2 tsp	1.5 oz plus 0.50 oz	42.5 g plus 14 g	Honey
½ tsp	0.1 oz	3 g	Salt
2 tbsp plus 2 tsp	0.96 oz plus 0.32 oz	27.25 g plus 9.08 g	Vegetable oil of your personal preference

Directions

1. Put the yeast into a large mixing bowl and add the water, stir to dissolve.
2. Add the honey to the yeast mixture and stir.

3. Add the whole wheat flour, vegetable oil, and salt to the mixing bowl and stir.

4. Add the all-purpose flour gradually to the dough mixture until you have added it all.

5. Scrape the dough out onto a lightly floured workspace and knead the dough for a minimum of 10-15 minutes.

6. When the dough is elastic and smooth, place the dough ball into an oiled bowl, and turn it around a few times to ensure that the entire surface of the dough is covered in oil and then cover the bowl with a damp kitchen cloth.

7. Place the bowl of dough in a warm part of the kitchen to rise for about 45 minutes until the dough has doubled in size.

8. Punch the dough down and then shape it into an oblong loaf and place it into the prepared loaf pan.

9. Set the pan aside to let the dough rise again until it is about 1 to 1 ½ inches above the rim of the pan.

10. Switch the oven on during the second rising phase to preheat to 375 degrees F (190 degrees C).

11. Place the loaf pan on the center rack of the oven and bake for 25-30 minutes, until bread is brown.

French Baguette

This baguette is easy and quick to make. You do not need any special equipment and it is built from everyday ingredients in your home, a budget-friendly baguette.

Time: 2 hours 20 minutes

Serving Size: 6 servings, makes 1 large loaf or 6 mini loaves

Prep Time: 20 minutes plus 1 hour 45 minutes for rising time

Cook Time: 15 minutes

Nutritional Facts/Info:

Calories 331.5

Carbs 60.8 g

Fat 5.4 g

Protein 8.6 g

Ingredients

3 ¼ cups	13.9 oz	394 g	All-purpose flour, plus extra if needed
1 tsp	0.14 oz	4 g	White sugar
2 tsp	0.22 oz	6 g	Active dry yeast
2 tbsp	0.96 oz	27.3 g	Vegetable oil
1 ½ tsp	0.3 oz	9 g	Salt
1 ½ cups	12 oz	345 g	Water, hot

Directions

1. Place the hot water and sugar into a 2-cup measure and stir to dissolve. Add the yeast and give the mixture a gentle stir. Allow the yeast to stand for about 5 minutes until it is foamy.

2. Place the salt and flour into a large mixing bowl and combine. Make a well in the center of the mixture and add the yeast mixture into the well. Use a wooden spoon and stir, starting in the middle until you have a sticky dough.

3. Knead the dough for about 10 minutes in the mixing bowl, adding small amounts of flour if needed until the dough is no longer sticky. The dough is ready when it is elastic.

4. Oil a deep mixing bowl and place the dough inside. Turn the dough over to make sure all surfaces are coated. Cover with plastic wrap or a damp kitchen cloth and set aside to rise for 1 hour.

5. Fill a large roasting pan with water and place it on the bottom rack in the oven. Line a baking sheet with parchment paper or a silicone baking mat and set aside. Preheat the oven to 425 degrees F (220 degrees C).

6. Punch the dough down in the mixing bowl and then place it on a floured work surface. You can shape the dough into one large oblong or oval loaf or divide it into six equal pieces for individual mini baguettes. Place the loaf or mini loaves onto the prepared baking sheet.

7. Score the bread by making four diagonal slashes across (mini loaves should have one diagonal slash). Cover with a dry kitchen cloth and allow to rise for 40 minutes until it has doubled in size.

8. Remove the kitchen cloth and place the baking sheet on the center rack in the oven and bake for between 15 to 20 minutes—time will depend on the size of loaf or loaves—until golden brown.

9. Place on a wire cooling rack to cool down for 10 minutes before slicing.

Chapter 8

Whole Wheat and Olive Oil Bread

———•✦•———

R ecipes for whole wheat bread and olive oil dough are an important part of any baker's repertoire of go-to recipes that taste great and appeal to everyone.

Classic Whole Wheat Loaf

This whole wheat bread is not dense at all. It is moist and has a very faint sweet taste.

Time: 3 hours 17 minutes

Serving Size: 1 slice (16 servings), makes 1 large loaf

Prep Time: 12 minutes plus 2 hours 25 minutes rising time

Cook Time: 35-40 minutes

Nutritional Facts/Info:

Calories 150

Carbs 24 g

Fat 3.5 g

Protein 5 g

Ingredients

1 to 1 ⅛ cups	8 oz to 9 oz	227 to 255 g	Lukewarm water
¼ cup	1.8 oz	50 g	Vegetable oil
¼ cup	3 oz	85 g	Honey, or maple syrup, or molasses
2 ½ tsp	0.24 oz	7.5 g	Instant Yeast or
2 ¼ tsp	0.25 oz	7 g	Active dry yeast dissolved in 2 tbsp of the water from the recipe
3 ½ cups	14 oz	397 g	White whole wheat flour
1 ¼ tsp	0.25 oz	7.5 g	Salt
¼ cup	0.99 oz	28 g	Nonfat dry milk

Directions

1. Combine all the ingredients for the bread in a large mixing bowl or the bowl of a stand mixer and stir until the dough starts pulling away from the sides of the bowl.

2. Let the dough rest for roughly 20-30 minutes. This is necessary to allow the flour to absorb liquid and also for the grain to soften. This will make it easier to knead the dough.

3. If using a stand mixer, use the dough hook and knead on low speed for 5-7 minutes until the dough is smooth. If kneading by hand, place the dough on a lightly floured surface and knead until the dough is supple and smooth about 6-8 minutes.

4. You can adjust the consistency of the dough during the kneading process if needed. If the dough stays very wet, you can add small amounts of flour until the consistency is better. If the dough feels too dry and stiff, you can add small amounts of water until you are satisfied with the consistency.

5. Place the kneaded dough in a greased bowl and cover with plastic wrap or a damp kitchen cloth and set aside to rise for 1-2 hours, until the dough is puffy. It does not have to exactly double in size.

6. Deflate the dough gently and then place it on a work surface that is lightly oiled. Shape the dough into a log of about 8 inches and place the dough log into a greased 8 ½ x 4 ½ x 2 ½ inches (21 x 11 x 6 cm) loaf pan. Cover the loaf pan with greased plastic wrap loosely.

7. Set the loaf pan in a warm place in the kitchen to rise for another 1-2 hours. The dough is ready once it has risen approximately 1 inch above the rim of the loaf pan.

8. About 30 minutes before the end of the rising time, switch on the oven and preheat to 350 degrees F (175 degrees C).

9. Remove the plastic wrap from the dough and place the baking pan in the center of the oven and bake for 35-40 minutes.

10. After 20 minutes of baking, make a loose tent of aluminum foil and place it over the bread in the oven to prevent the loaf from browning too fast.

11. The bread is done with the internal temperature reads at least 190 degrees F (88 degrees C) on a digital thermometer.

12. If you prefer a soft crust, rub the top of the bread with a stick of butter when you remove it from the oven.

13. Place the bread on a cooling rack and allow to cool down completely before slicing and serving.

14. The bread will stay fresh for several days if kept wrapped in a container at room temperature and it can be frozen as well.

Whole Wheat Potato Loaf

The combination of whole wheat, mashed potatoes, and all-purpose flour gives this bread a moist texture and it will stay fresh for quite a few days after baking.

Time: 3 hours

Serving Size: 1 slice (12 servings) makes 1 loaf

Prep Time: 25 minutes plus 2 hours rising time

Cook Time: 35 minutes

Nutritional Facts/Info:

Calories 132.4

Carbs 23.2 g

Fat 2.9 g

Protein 4.2 g

Ingredients

1 ¼ cups	6.2 oz	150 g	Whole wheat flour
1 cup	4 ¼ oz	120 g	All-purpose flour
1 ¼ tsp	0.25 oz	7.5 g	Salt
¾ cup	1.35 oz	38 g	Instant mashed potato flakes
2 ¼ tsp	0.25 oz	7 g	Active dry yeast (1 packet)
2 tbsp	1 ½ oz	42 g	Honey
½ cup plus 2 tbsp	4 oz plus 1 oz	118 g plus 28 g	Milk, warm
¾ cup	6 oz	177 g	Water, warm
1			Eggs, whisked
2 tbsp	1 oz	28 g	Margarine or butter

Directions

1. Place the potato flakes, all-purpose flour, salt, and yeast into a large mixing bowl and mix.

2. Put the water, margarine, milk, egg, and honey into a separate mixing bowl and whisk to blend.

3. Add the liquid to the dry ingredients and beat with a wooden spoon to combine.

4. Gradually add the whole wheat flour and mix until all the ingredients are evenly moistened.

5. Turn the dough out onto a lightly floured workspace and knead for about 5 minutes.

6. Place the dough into a greased bowl, cover with plastic wrap or a damp kitchen cloth and set aside to rise for about 1 hour until the dough has doubled in size.

7. Halfway during the rising phase, switch on the oven and preheat to 375 degrees F (190 degrees C).

8. Grease a loaf pan of 9 x 5 x 3 inches (23 x 13 x 8 cm) and set aside.

9. Punch down the dough and shape into an oblong form and place it into the greased loaf pan.

10. Bake the bread until it is light brown, about 35 minutes, and do the test for doneness by knocking on the bottom of the bread and listening for the hollow sound.

11. Place the bread on a cooling rack and allow to cool to room temperature before serving.

Olive Oil Bread

This is a simple, and easy bread to make and has a distinctive olive oil taste that goes well with all Italian dishes and pasta.

Time: 1 hour 45 minutes

Serving Size: 1 slice (15 servings) makes 1 loaf

Prep Time: 15 minutes plus 50 minutes rising time

Cook Time: 40 minutes

Nutritional Facts/Info:

Calories 110.5

Carbs 16.4 g

Fat 3.8 g

Protein 2.4 g

Ingredients

2 ½ cups	10.6 oz	300g	All-purpose flour	
½ cup	4 oz	118 g	Warm water (110 degrees F, 45 degrees C)	
1 tsp	0.14 oz	4 g	White sugar	
2 ¼ tsp	0.25 oz	7 g	Active dry yeast	
4 tbsp	1.88 oz	53 g	Olive oil	
1 tsp	0.2 oz	6 g	Salt	

Directions

1. Put the yeast and warm water into a mixing bowl and stir to dissolve the yeast. Add the sugar, olive oil, and salt.

2. Add 2 cups of flour and stir with a wooden spoon until it forms a soft ball of dough. Then slowly add the rest of the flour and knead it into the dough until the dough is no longer sticky.

3. Place the dough into a greased bowl and cover. Set it aside to rise until the dough has doubled in size, about 30 minutes.

4. Place the dough onto a lightly floured work surface and punch the dough down and then shape it into a round ball, or an into an oval shape. Place dough onto a greased baking sheet and cover. Leave to rise for an additional 15-20 minutes.

5. At the time you set the dough aside for the second rising, switch on the oven, and preheat to 375 degrees F (190 degrees C).

6. Bake the bread until it is golden brown, about 30-40 minutes.

7. Place on a wire cooling rack and allow to cool down for at least 10 minutes before slicing.

Olive Oil Rolls

These bread rolls are soft and great for dinner rolls and for sandwich bread buns.

Time: 4 hours 30 minutes

Serving Size: 1 bread roll (12 servings), makes 12 rolls

Prep Time: 15 minutes plus 4 hours for the dough to rise

Cook Time: 15 minutes

Nutritional Facts/Info:

Calories 109

Carbs 16 g

Fat 3 g

Protein 2 g

Ingredients

2 cups	8.8 oz	250 g	Flour, bread or all-purpose
½ tsp	0.05 oz	1.4 g	Active dry yeast
½ tsp	0.1 oz	2.85 g	Salt
½ cup plus 3 tbsp	5.7 oz	162 g	Lukewarm water
3 tbsp	1.4 oz	40 g	Olive oil
¾ tsp	0.19	5.3 g	Honey

Directions

1. Put the water and honey in a small bowl and sprinkle the dry yeast into the water mixture. Set aside for 5 minutes and then stir to combine.

2. Place the flour and salt into the bowl of a stand mixer and whisk to mix the salt through the flour evenly. Switch to the dough hook and make a well in the middle of the bowl and add the yeast mixture.

3. Knead the dough with the dough hook for about 10-12 minutes, until the dough forms a ball. Stop a few times during the kneading to scrape the sides of the bowl clean and remove dough from the hook.

4. Lightly dust a work surface with flour and knead it by hand for 2-3 minutes. Then place the dough ball into a greased mixing bowl and roll the ball around to coat the surface with oil.

5. Cover the bowl and leave in a warm area in the kitchen to rise for 2 hours until the dough has doubled in size.

6. Remove the dough and place it on the floured work surface again and punch it down.

7. Make 12 evenly sized balls of dough or alternatively you can roll out the dough in a rectangular shape and roll up, and then cut into 12 rolled up balls. Keep the dough covered while you make the balls to prevent it from drying out.

8. Place the dough balls into a baking sheet that has been lined with parchment paper. Cover the rolls with a damp cloth and leave to rise until rolls have doubled in size again, about 1 hour.

9. Preheat the oven during the second rising time to 400 degrees F (200 degrees C).

10. Brush the dough balls with olive oil using a pastry brush, before placing the rolls into the oven.

11. Bake the rolls until they are golden brown, for 10-15 minutes. Test to see if they are done by knocking on the bottom to hear the hollow sound that means it is done.

12. Place on a cooling rack to cool down for about 10 minutes before serving.

Chapter 9

Vegan and Gluten-Free

Many people follow special diets and it is always good to have basic recipes on hand to cater to vegetarian, vegan, and gluten intolerant people, especially when it comes to entertaining.

Easy White Bread (Gluten-Free)

This is the perfect go-to recipe for gluten-free bread and easy to make. You can have this bread ready in just 2 hours and it's a great help when you have to cater for gluten intolerant people. An extra bonus is that this is no-knead bread.

Time: 2 hours 5 minutes

Serving Size: 1 slice (8 servings), makes 1 loaf

Prep Time: 10 minutes plus 1 hour 10 minutes for the dough to rise

Cook Time: 45 minutes

Nutritional Facts/Info:

Calories 179.9

Carbs 26.8 g

Fat 7.1 g

Protein 5 g

Ingredients

2 cups	8 ½ oz	240 g	Gluten-free all-purpose flour
2 tsp	0.22 oz	6 g	Active dry yeast
2 tbsp	0.96 oz	27 g	Sunflower oil
1			Egg white
1			Egg
⅞ cup	7.3 oz	207 g	Water, warm
1 tbsp	0.51 oz	14.4 g	Apple cider vinegar
2 tsp	0.52 oz	14.8 g	Xanthan gum

Directions

1. Put the yeast into a small mixing bowl and add the warm water. Allow this to stand for about 10 minutes, until the yeast has started to be foamy.
2. Add the egg white, the whole egg, vinegar, and oil and whisk until the ingredients are blended.
3. Prepare a 2-lb loaf pan (8 x 4 x 3 inches) (21 x 11 x 7 cm) with vegetable oil or cooking spray and set aside.

4. Sift the xanthan gum and flour together and place in the bowl of a stand mixer and fit the paddle attachment.

5. Add the yeast mixture to the bowl slowly while mixing at low speed. Then switch to medium speed and mix until you have a smooth batter.

6. Pour the bread batter into the greased loaf pan and see that the top of the loaf is smooth.

7. Cover the loaf pan with a damp kitchen towel or oiled plastic wrap and set aside to rise for 1 hour, until the bread batter had doubled in size.

8. Switch on the stove about 30 minutes into the rising time and preheat to 375 degrees F (190 degrees C).

9. Bake the bread for 45 minutes, until it is golden brown. Remove the bread from the pan and tap on the bottom and if the sound is hollow the bread is done.

10. Place the loaf on a cooling rack and allow to cool down completely before slicing and serving.

Multigrain Loaf (Gluten-Free)

This multigrain gluten-free bread has a very good texture, it holds together very well making it a versatile loaf for eating just with butter, for sandwiches, and for toast.

Time: 2 hours 30 minutes

Serving Size: 1 slice (10 servings), produces 1 loaf

Prep Time: 20 minutes plus 1 hour 30 minutes rising time

Cook Time: 45 minutes

Nutritional Facts/Info:

Calories 230

Carbs 28.5 g

Fat 10.5 g

Protein 6.7 g

Ingredients

¾ cup	4.18 oz	118.5 g	Brown rice flour
1 tsp	0.02 oz	4.7 g	Butter, or as needed
¼ cup	1.13 oz	32 g	Tapioca starch
1 tsp	0.2 oz	6 g	Salt
¼ cup	1.7 oz	48 g	Potato starch
1 tsp	0.1 oz	4 g	Baking powder
2 tsp	0.22 oz	6 g	Active dry yeast
¼ cup	1.9 oz	50 g	Quinoa
2 tsp	0.24 oz	6.7 g	Guar gum
¼ cup	1.1 oz	31.5 g	Almonds, toasted and chopped
¾ cup	6 oz	177 g	Milk, warm (115 degrees F, 46 degrees C)
2			Egg whites

2			Eggs
2 tbsp	1.48 oz	42 g	Agave nectar
2 tbsp	1.49 oz	42 g	Molasses
2 tbsp	0.94 oz	26.6 g	Olive oil
1 tsp	0.11 oz	3.04 g	Sesame seeds
2 tsp	0.338 oz	9.58 g	Apple cider vinegar
¼ cup	1.16 oz	43.5 g	Sunflower seed
¼ cup	1.44 oz	42.25 g	Flax seed

Directions

1. Grease and flour a 9 x 5 x 3 inches (23 x 13 x 8 cm) loaf pan and set aside.
2. Sift the tapioca starch, yeast, baking powder, potato starch, guar gum, and rice flour into a large mixing bowl.
3. Put the flax seed, quinoa, almonds, and sunflower seed into a coffee grinder and grind into a very fine powder and add this to the flour mixture.
4. Place the vinegar, milk, olive oil, eggs, agave nectar, molasses, and egg whites into the bowl of a stand mixer.

Fit the paddle attachment and beat the ingredients until blended well using the low-speed setting.

5. Add the dry ingredients a few spoons at a time to the wet ingredients using the medium-high speed until all the ingredients are well combined. Use a spatula to push down the dough as needed.

6. Scrape the dough into the prepared loaf pan with a spatula and even out the top with a wet spatula. Sprinkle the sesame seeds over the top of the dough.

7. Boil a kettle of water, then fill a large bowl with the hot water. Place this bowl inside a microwave and place a cooling rack over the bowl. Then place the loaf pan on top of the cooling rack. Cover the dough with a kitchen cloth and close the microwave oven door.

8. Let the bread dough rise for 1 hour 30 minutes until the dough has risen to the rim of the loaf pan.

9. An hour into the rising time, switch on the oven and preheat to 350 degrees F (175 degrees C).

10. Bake for about 45 minutes until the crust is golden brown. Test for doneness by inserting an instant-read thermometer into the bread, the temperature should read 200 degrees F (93 degrees C).

11. Place the bread on a wire cooling rack and allow it to cool down completely and use a serrated edge knife to slice the bread.

Zucchini Bread (Vegan)

This is a soft bread with a fluffy texture and tastes great on its own or served with vegan butter and maple syrup. This loaf can be stored at room temperature, in an airtight container for up to 5 days. This bread also freezes well for up to 1 month.

Time: 1 hour 20 minutes

Serving Size: 1 slice (10 servings), yields 1 loaf

Prep Time: 15 minutes

Cook Time: 65 minutes

Nutritional Facts/Info:

Calories 233

Carbs 35 g

Fat 9 g

Protein 2 g

Ingredients

1 ½ cups	6.4 oz	187.5 g	All-purpose flour
1 cup	8.82 oz	250 g	Applesauce, unsweetened
½ tsp	0.04 oz	1.2 g	Nutmeg
⅓ cup	2.35 oz	68 g	Brown sugar, packed
½ tsp	0.1 oz	3 g	Salt
¼ cup	1.74 oz	49.5 g	Vegetable oil
1 tsp	0.09 oz	2.64 g	Cinnamon, ground
1 tsp	0.15 oz	4.2 g	Vanilla extract
1 tsp	0.21	6 g	Baking soda
1 ¼ cups	6.6 oz	190 g	Zucchini, shredded
½ tsp	0.05 oz	2 g	Baking powder
½ cup	3 ½ oz	99 g	White sugar

⅛ tsp	0.088 oz	0.25 g	Cardamom
½ cup	2.2 oz	63 g	Walnuts, chopped

Directions

1. Spray a 8 x 4 x 2 ½ inch (20 x 10 x 6 cm) loaf pan with vegetable oil and set aside.

2. Preheat the oven to 350 degrees (175 degrees C).

3. Shred 1 medium zucchini with a handheld shredder or use the shredding attachment if you have a food processor. Squeeze out all the excess liquid from the zucchini by straining it through a fine-mesh strainer or through a piece of cheesecloth and set aside.

4. Put the applesauce, white and brown sugar, vanilla extract, and vegetable oil into a large mixing bowl and whisk.

5. Place the spices, baking powder, flour, salt, and baking soda into a separate bowl and combine. Add the dry ingredients to the bowl holding the wet ingredients and stir until all the ingredients are combined.

6. Lastly, fold in the walnuts and the shredded zucchini.

7. Spoon the batter into the prepared loaf pan and bake until a toothpick inserted into the loaf comes out clean, about 50-65 minutes.

8. Let the bread cool down in the pan for a minimum of 10 minutes before transferring the loaf to a wire cooling rack to cool down completely before slicing.

Sorghum Whole Wheat Bread (Vegan)

This is a very easy and simple no-knead recipe, you just have to punch down the dough and it's baked in a Dutch oven.

Time: 5 hours 35 minutes

Serving Size: 1 slice (12 servings), yields 1 round loaf

Prep Time: 20 minutes, plus 3 hours 30 minutes rising time, plus 1 hour cooling time

Cook Time: 40 minutes

Nutritional Facts/Info:

Calories 132.9

Carbs 28 g

Fat 0.4 g

Protein 5 g

Ingredients

1 ⅛ tsp	0.125 oz	3.5 g	Active dry yeast (½ packet)
2 cups plus 2 tbsp	8 ½ oz plus 0.54 oz	240 g plus 15.2 g	Whole wheat flour, divided
1 ½ cups	12 oz	345 g	Lukewarm water plus extra if needed
1 tsp	0.2 oz	6 g	Salt
1 ½ cups	6/41 oz	182 g	Sorghum flour

Directions

1. Put the yeast into a small mixing bowl and add 1 ½ cups of lukewarm water. Stir to dissolve and set aside for about 5 minutes until the yeast is foamy.
2. Place the sorghum flour, 2 cups of whole wheat flour, and salt into a very large plastic bowl with a lid.
3. Stir the yeast mixture into the dry ingredients with a wooden spoon. If the liquid is not enough to moisten the dough evenly, add extra water a little at a time.

4. Cover the bowl with the lid and place in a draft-free and warm part of the kitchen for about 2 hours until the dough has doubled in size.

5. Dust a cutting board or a workspace with 1 tbsp of whole wheat flour. Turn the dough out onto the floured board and punch the dough down, kneading it for only a few minutes.

6. Shape the dough into a round loaf by hand and then sprinkle the rest of the whole wheat flour over a clean, lint-free kitchen cloth. Place this cloth inside a deep bowl and then put the shaped dough ball into this bowl. Fold the ends of the kitchen cloth over the dough and allow the dough to rise for about 1 ½ hours until it has doubled in size again.

7. Switch on the oven about 45 minutes into the second rising of the dough and preheat to 450 degrees F (230 degrees C).

8. Place the lidded Dutch oven into the oven 25 minutes after switching on the oven.

9. Use oven mitts to remove the Dutch oven from the stove oven and set on a wooden cutting board and remove the lid.

10. Lift the risen dough out of the bowl by the ends of the kitchen cloth. Flour your hands before you remove the

dough from the kitchen cloth, then carefully place the dough into the Dutch oven and put the lid on.

11. Place the Dutch oven back into the stove and bake for 30 minutes. Then remove the lid from the Dutch oven and continue baking uncovered for another 10 minutes until the bread is golden brown.

12. Remove the Dutch oven using oven mitts and tap the bottom of the loaf to do the doneness test. When the sound is hollow place the bread on a cooling rack.

13. Leave the bread to cool down for at least 1 hour before serving.

Chapter 10

Sourdough

Sourdough bread has become very popular again as people like the different taste that is not like the taste of bread made with commercial yeast. Sourdough bread has a tang that other yeast bread does not have at all. People now find the tangy taste refreshing from other yeast bread, so it is always good to include sourdough bread in your repertoire when you start out baking.

Sourdough Starter Terminology

The following are a few of the terms you will learn when you make your own sourdough starter. They may be confusing in the beginning, so we will go over the most common terms here.

Levain

This is another word that actually refers to a pre-ferment that contains bacteria and wild yeast. As the sourdough starter is made from wild yeast, people often refer to it as a levain.

Ripen

This is when the lactobacillus and yeasts are allowed to develop the starter to maturity.

Hooch

This is the alcohol layer that develops on top of the starter. It is not harmful at all but can affect the flavor of your starter, so it is always advised to pour that off before feeding the starter.

Wild Yeast Starter

A leavening agent made from naturally occurring bacteria and yeasts that can be found on grain and in the air around us. So, when water and flour are mixed and then left to ferment, it is called a wild yeast starter.

Feeding a Starter

You feed a starter by adding equal weights of water and flour to the starter daily to keep it active if you keep your starter at room temperature. Refrigerator starters only get fed once per week, so it is less work.

Maintaining a Starter

This refers to a person feeding a starter to keep it healthy and also by keeping the starter at the best temperature for it to stay alive.

Lactobacilli

This bacteria is also referred to as lactic acid bacteria (LAB) and during the rising of dough lactic acid combines with acetic acid and this gives sourdough bread its distinctive tang.

To increase the sour taste in sourdough bread people keep their starter in the refrigerator because the cold encourages the forming of more acetic acid and slows down the forming of lactic acid.

Sourdough Discard

Every time the starter is fed, you have to remove half of the original starter before feeding it. This is called the discard, which is a bit of a misnomer as you do not have to throw away the discard. You use this to bake with or to pass on to a friend or acquaintance to start their own sourdough starter.

Sourdough Starter Kit

A sourdough starter can be created either through starting your own from scratch or buying a commercially available sourdough culture kit. These starter kits are available as a fresh live culture or can be bought in a dehydrated form and then reactivated at home.

Sourdough Starter

This is what sourdough bread is all about, the 'magic' ingredient that turns ordinary bread into delicious, tangy sourdough bread and buns.

Time: 1 week 3 days

Serving Size: 8 servings

Prep Time: 15 minutes

Cook Time: n/a

Nutritional Facts/Info:

Calories 316

Carbs 63.5 g

Fat 1.5 g

Protein 10.5 g

Ingredients

5 cups	⅓	1 ½ lbs	680 g	Bread flour
2.87 cups		1 ½ lbs	680 g	Water - cool water if your home is warm and lukewarm water if your home is cool

Directions

1. Day 1: Mix ½ cup (2 oz) (60 g) bread flour and ¼ cup (2 oz) (60g) water.

2. Combine the bread flour and water in a non-reactive container with at least 1-quart (1 liter) capacity. Stainless steel, crockery, food-grade plastic, or glass is best suited for this. The size of the container is important as it should allow space for the growth of the starter.

3. Stir the water and flour well and make sure there are no dry flour lumps at all. Cover the container, but do not seal it. Allow the mixture to sit for 24 hours at 70 degrees F (21 degrees C).

4. Day 2: Add ½ cup (2 oz) (60 g) bread flour and ¼ cup (2 oz) (60g) water to the container holding the starter and stir. Cover the container and leave for 24 hours at 70 degrees F (21 degrees C).

5. Day 3: Remove half of the starter, roughly 5 oz (140 g). Add ½ cup (2 oz) (60 g) bread flour and ¼ cup (2 oz) (60g)

water to the container holding the starter and sir. Cover the container and leave for 24 hours at 70 degrees F (21 degrees C).

6. Day 4 up to, and including day 10: Repeat day 3 every day. By day 10 the sourdough starter should have a yeasty and fruity smell. The starter is ready if it doubles in size within 2-3 hours after it was fed.

7. Once the starter is complete you can keep it in the refrigerator. A starter stored in the refrigerator should be fed once every week.

8. When you want to bake sourdough bread, remove the starter from the fridge and feed it at room temperature for 2 days, this will refresh the starter. Use the refreshed starter to bake with on the 3rd day.

9. Remember to keep 5 oz (140 g) starter aside and feed it before placing it back into the fridge.

10. If your house is very cold, place the container of starter on or near an appliance that gives off heat so that the temperature is as close to 70 degrees F (21 degrees C) as possible.

Everyday Sourdough Bread

When you start baking sourdough bread, this loaf is your go-to basic sourdough loaf with no frills or any difficult steps

Time: 3 hours 30 minutes

Serving Size: 1 slice (18 servings), makes 1 loaf

Prep Time: 10 minutes plus 2 hours 30 minutes rising time

Cook Time: 40-50 minutes

Nutritional Facts/Info:

Calories 110

Carbs 23 g

Fat 0 g

Protein 4 g

Ingredients

2 ½ cups	10.6 oz	300 g	All-purpose flour
2 cups	16 oz	454 g	Sourdough starter, fed and ripe
1 ½ tsp	0.21 oz	6 g	Sugar
½ cup	4 oz	118 g	Water, lukewarm
1 ½ tsp	0.3 oz	9 g	Salt

Directions

1. Combine all the ingredients in a large mixing bowl or the bowl of a stand mixer or food processor.

2. Knead the dough by hand for 15-20 minutes on a floured surface, or for 7-10 minutes in a stand mixer or food processor using the dough hook. The dough is ready when it has a smooth and soft texture.

3. Grease a bowl and place the dough inside. Set the bowl aside for 45-60 minutes for the dough to rise. The risen dough should be puffy, but not necessarily have doubled in size.

4. Grease a 9 x 5 x 3 inches (23 x 13 x 8 cm) loaf pan and set aside.

5. Place the dough ball on a floured surface and gently punch the dough down to deflate.

6. Form the dough into a log of about 9 inches and place it into the prepared pan.

7. Cover the pan with a kitchen cloth or plastic wrap and allow the dough to rise for 60-90 minutes. The dough should have risen about 1 inch above the rim of the bread pan.

8. Switch on the oven 60 minutes into the second rising and preheat to 350 degrees F (175 degrees C).

9. Bake the bread until it has a light golden color, for 40-50 minutes. The bread is done when you insert a digital thermometer into the center, and it reads 190 degrees F (88 degrees C).

10. Remove the bread from the oven and allow it to cool down in the pan for about 5 minutes and then place on a cooling rack to cool to room temperature before serving.

11. This bread can be stored well-wrapped for a number of days at room temperature. It can also be frozen for up to 3 months.

Cracked Wheat Bread

This loaf has great flavor from different flours and several different types of seeds. Please note that this bread has three rising periods whereas most bread loaves only require two rising periods.

Time: 4 hours 30 minutes

Serving Size: 1 slice (12 servings), yields 1 loaf

Prep Time: 30 minutes, plus 3 hours 30 minutes rising time

Cook Time: 30 minutes

Nutritional Facts/Info:

Calories 199.9

Carbs 36.1 g

Fat 3.9 g

Protein 7.4 g

Ingredients

¼ cup plus 2 tbsp	1.1 oz plus 0.52 oz	45 g	Cracked wheat
1 cup	4 ¼ oz	120 g	Whole wheat flour
1 ¾ cups	5 ⅓ oz	150 g	Bread flour
1 ¼ cup	10 oz	284 g	Sourdough starter
½ cup	4 oz	118 g	Water, hot
¼ cup	1.44 oz	42.3 g	Flax seeds
¼ cup	1.16 oz	43.5 g	Sunflower seeds, raw
2 tbsp	1 oz	28 g	Margarine, melted
½			Egg, whisked
1 tbsp	0.74 oz	21.1 g	Molasses
1 tbsp	¾ oz	21 g	Honey

¼ cup plus 2 tbsp	3 oz	87 g	Nonfat milk

Directions

1. Place the cracked wheat into a medium-sized bowl and pour the hot water over it. (Please note that the water does not need to be at the boiling point, just hot).

2. Add the flax seeds, melted margarine, nonfat milk, sunflower seeds, honey, and molasses and mix through. Set the bowl aside to cool down to lukewarm.

3. Once the contents of the bowl have cooled to lukewarm add the sourdough starter and stir.

4. Add the flours gradually 1 cup at a time. Start off with the whole wheat and then the bread flour and use a sturdy wooden spoon to stir.

5. When the dough is stiff enough to hold together, turn it out onto a lightly floured work surface and knead for 10-12 minutes. Add some of the remaining flour if necessary, but it is not essential that you use all the flour.

6. Once the dough is elastic and smooth, use your hands to shape it into a ball.

7. Place the dough ball into a greased bowl and cover.

8. Leave the bowl in a draft-free place in the kitchen for 1 ½ hours until the dough has doubled in size.

9. Punch the dough down and again cover the dough with a kitchen cloth or plastic wrap. Allow the dough to rise for a second time for about 1 hour until it has again risen to double the size.

10. Punch the dough down again and shape the dough into an oblong log and place it into a greased 9 x 5 x 3 inches (23 x 13 8 cm) loaf pan. Set the loaf pan aside for the dough to rise for the third time for 1 hour.

11. Make an egg wash of 1 tbsp of water and 1 whole egg, whisked well, and brush the top of the loaf with the egg wash using a pastry brush.

12. Switch the oven on about 30 minutes before the end of the third rising session and preheat to 375 degrees F (190 degrees C).

13. Bake the bread for about 30 minutes, after 15 minutes spray the pan with cold water and continue baking. The bread is done when it makes a hollow sound when you tap your knuckles on the bottom of the loaf.

14. Place the loaf pan on a cooling rack and allow the bread to cool down in the pan for 10 minutes before removing the loaf. Then place the loaf on the cooling rack to cool down completely before slicing.

Pumpkin Spice Sourdough Loaf

This spicy sourdough bread is easy to make, does not require extra time for rising, plus does not get kneaded at all. This bread will stay fresh for several days in an airtight container at room temperature and can be frozen for up to 3 months as well.

Time: 1 hour 15 minutes to 1 hour 45 minutes

Serving Size: ½ slice (16 servings), yields 1 loaf

Prep Time: 15 minutes

Cook Time: 1 hour to 1 hour 30 minutes

Nutritional Facts/Info:

Calories 200

Carbs 30 g

Fat 8 g

Protein 4 g

Ingredients

2 cups	8 ½ oz	240 g	All-purpose flour
¾ cup	6 oz	170g	Sourdough starter unfed/discard
⅓ cup	2.36 oz	67 g	Vegetable oil
½ tsp	0.03 oz	0.88 g	Ginger
½ cup	3 ½ oz	99 g	Sugar
½ tsp	0.04 oz	1.10 g	Cloves
¼ cup	3 oz	85 g	Molasses
¼ tsp	0.02 oz	0.59 g	Nutmeg
2			Eggs, large
½ tsp	0.05 oz	2 g	Baking powder
1 cup	8 oz	227 g	Pumpkin purée
½ tsp	0.10 oz	3 g	Baking soda
1 tsp	0.15 oz	4.2 g	Vanilla extract

½ cup	2 oz	57 g	Walnuts, chopped
¾ tsp	0.15 oz	4.5 g	Salt
½ cup	3 oz	85 g	Raisins
½ tsp	0.05 oz	1.32 g	Cinnamon

Directions

1. Grease a 9 x 5 x 3 inches (23 x 13 x 8 cm) loaf pan and set aside. Switch on the oven and preheat to 350 degrees F (175 degrees C).

2. Place the sugar, pumpkin, oil, eggs, and molasses into a large mixing bowl and stir. Add the vanilla and the sourdough starter and stir again.

3. In a separate bowl, whisk the baking soda, flour, baking powder, salt, and spices together.

4. Add the dry ingredients to the bowl holding the wet ingredients and combine until all the ingredients are blended.

5. Stir the raisins and the nuts into the batter.

6. Pour the batter into the prepared loaf pan and place it into the oven.

7. Bake for 60-65 minutes and do a test for doneness by inserting a paring knife into the center of the loaf. If it comes out clean, the bread is done.

8. Remove from the oven and place the loaf pan on a cooling rack and allow the bread to cool down in the pan for 15 minutes before turning the loaf out onto the cooling rack.

9. Allow the pumpkin bread to cool completely before it is sliced.

Sourdough Bread Sticks

These breadsticks contain a sourdough starter as well as active dry yeast that creates perfect breadsticks. These freeze extremely well, making this recipe perfect for batch baking.

Time: 2 hours 35 minutes

Serving Size: 1 breadstick (6 servings)

Prep Time: 25 minutes plus 1 hour 50 minutes rising time

Cook Time: 20 to 30 minutes

Nutritional Facts/Info:

Calories 200.1

Carbs 40.9 g

Fat 0.9 g

Protein 6.3 g

Ingredients

2 cups	8 ½ oz	240 g	All-purpose flour
½ cup	4 oz	227 g	Sourdough starter
½ tsp	0.05 oz	1.5 g	Active dry yeast
½ cup	4 oz	118 g	Water, warm, plus more if needed
1 tbsp plus 1 ½ tsp	0.64 oz	18 g	White sugar, divided
½ tsp	0.1 oz	3 g	Salt
1/2			Egg, separated
			Cooking spray of own choice

Directions

1. Place half the sugar and water into a bowl and dissolve. Add yeast and set aside 5-10 minutes until the mixture is foamy.
2. Put the rest of the sugar, salt, and flour into a large mixing bowl and mix.

3. Put the egg yolk and sourdough starter in a separate bowl and combine. Put the egg white in a separate bowl and whisk and place it in the refrigerator until needed.

4. Add the sourdough and the yeast mixture to the dry ingredients. Use a wooden spoon and mix until all the ingredients are blended and the mixture holds together in a soft dough.

5. Turn the dough out onto a floured surface and knead until it forms a smooth dough for about 10-15 minutes.

6. Spray a large bowl with the vegetable oil and place the dough ball into the bowl and cover with a cloth or plastic wrap and allow the dough to rise for about 1 hour.

7. Punch the dough down and divide it into six equal-sized pieces. Roll the dough balls into breadsticks of about 3-4 inches (7.6-10 cm) long. Place the breadsticks onto a baking sheet lined with parchment paper and cover with a cloth. Set aside to rest for 45 minutes.

8. Preheat the oven to 350 degrees F (175 degrees C).

9. Bake the breadsticks for 15-20 minutes until light brown. Remove the baking pan from the oven and brush the tops with egg white using a pastry brush. Return to the oven and continue baking for 5-10 minutes until the breadsticks are medium brown.

10. Allow to cool down on a cooling rack for about 10 minutes before serving with toppings of your own choice.

Conclusion

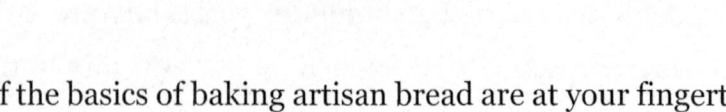

All of the basics of baking artisan bread are at your fingertips now. Your do's and don'ts section is an important part of everything, refresh your memory by going over it once in a while. Think about those who had made the mistakes and smile, they are saving you from a lot of frustration.

The most important thing to take from this book is that there is no such thing as cannot. With the correct information, the right tools, and your determination you are able to tackle every type of artisan loaf as your experience grows. Start with the easy and basic loaves and once you have mastered these you will have a rock-solid foundation on which to build your mastery of the most intricate recipes.

So what if occasionally there is a rough spot, a few hiccups, it really does not matter at all. Make bread crumbs of the flops to use in other cooking and keep going! Baking artisan bread is a journey of discovery, with a few small stones on the path. Kick them aside, and have fun creating great tasting goodies everyone will love.

References

Ajale. (2017, February 4). *Dough sourdough pity – Free photo on Pixabay.* Pixabay. [Image]. https://pixabay.com/photos/dough-sourdough-pity-bread-baking-2073691/

Alkier, D. (2019, July 1). *Pastry bread beside red sauce photo – Free cutlery image on Unsplash.* [Image]. Unsplash. https://unsplash.com/photos/_8isFizCcvQ

Amyw. (n.d.). *Effortless Rustic Bread.* Allrecipes. https://www.allrecipes.com/recipe/244916/effortless-rustic-bread

Anaterate. (2017, August 1). *Bread whole wheat – Free photo on Pixabay.* Pixabay. [Image]. https://pixabay.com/photos/bread-whole-wheat-bread-bread-slices-2568302/

Argo, Karo, & Fleischmann's. (n.d.). *Classic Dinner Rolls.* Allrecipes. https://www.allrecipes.com/recipe/215378/classic-dinner-rolls/

Babuschka. (n.d.). *No-Knead Whole Wheat Bread with Sorghum Flour.* Allrecipes. https://www.allrecipes.com/recipe/260354/no-knead-whole-wheat-bread-with-sorghum-flour/

Baier, L. (2018, February 21). *Differences Between Types of Yeast.* https://www.asweetpeachef.com/differences-between-types-of-yeast/.

Barr, A. (n.d.). *Italian Herb Bread I.* Allrecipes. https://www.allrecipes.com/recipe/6784/italian-herb-bread-i/

Basic Sourdough Bread | King Arthur Flour. (n.d.). Www.Kingarthurflour.com. https://www.kingarthurflour.com/recipes/basic-sourdough-bread-recipe

Beck, A. (n.d.) *These 21 Baking Tools Are Absolutely Essential.* https://www.bhg.com/recipes/how-to/bake/essential-baking-tools.

Boldt, A. (n.d.). *What Are the Health Benefits of Baking Your Own Bread?* Livestrong.com. https://www.livestrong.com/article/344384-what-are-the-health-benefits-of-baking-your-own-bread/

Carol. (n.d.-b). *Raisin Bread I.* Allrecipes. https://www.allrecipes.com/recipe/6936/raisin-bread-i/

Cathy W. (n.d.-d). *Bread baking terms from A-C.* Bread Experience. https://www.breadexperience.com/bread-baking-terms/

Chef John. (n.d.). *Chef John's Sourdough Starter.* Allrecipes. https://www.allrecipes.com/recipe/260539/chef-johns-sourdough-starter/

Classic 100% Whole Wheat Bread | King Arthur Flour. (n.d.). Www.Kingarthurflour.Com. https://www.kingarthurflour.com/recipes/classic-100-whole-wheat-bread-recipe

Classic Sandwich Bread | King Arthur Flour. (n.d.). Www.Kingarthurflour.Com. https://www.kingarthurflour.com/recipes/classic-sandwich-bread-recipe

Cook, D. (n.d.). *Perfect Sourdough Bread Sticks*. Allrecipes. https://www.allrecipes.com/recipe/272531/perfect-sourdough-bread-sticks/

Counselling. (2015, April 1). *Kitchen appliances spoon pancake – Free photo on Pixabay.* Pixabay. [Image]. https://pixabay.com/photos/kitchen-appliances-spoon-pancake-701128/

DDP. (2019, April 7). *Person baking pastry photo – Free bread image on Unsplash.* Unsplash. [Image]. https://unsplash.com/photos/aNz2IUoWCAg

Dee. (n.d.-c). *Olive Oil Bread*. Allrecipes. https://www.allrecipes.com/recipe/17804/olive-oil-bread/

Giulioperricone. (2019, July 2). *Flour dough kneed – Free photo on Pixabay.* Pixabay. [Image]. https://pixabay.com/photos/flour-dough-knead-kitchen-food-4310465/

Griffiths, M. (2017a, July 13). *Easy Homemade Subway Bread | Subway Copycat Recipe.* Bless This Mess.

https://www.blessthismessplease.com/homemade-subway-bread-recipe#tasty-recipes-22439

Jaclyn. (n.d.). *Cracked Wheat Sourdough Bread*. Allrecipes. https://www.allrecipes.com/recipe/7225/cracked-wheat-sourdough-bread/

Kamila211. (2016, December 14). *No-glutren bread gluten free – free photo on Pixabay*. Pixabay. [Image]. https://pixabay.com/photos/no-gluten-bread-gluten-free-bread-1905736/

Keri. (n.d.). *Jim's Cheddar Onion Soda Bread*. Allrecipes. https://www.allrecipes.com/recipe/216934/jims-cheddar-onion-soda-bread

Loló. (n.d.). *Gluten-Free White Bread*. Allrecipes. https://www.allrecipes.com/recipe/264166/gluten-free-white-bread/

McMinn, S. (2018, May 23). *Best-Ever Vegan Zucchini Bread*. My Darling Vegan. https://www.mydarlingvegan.com/vegan-zucchini-bread/

Monahan, M. (n.d.). *Honey Wheat Bread II*. Allrecipes. https://www.allrecipes.com/recipe/6763/honey-wheat-bread-ii/

Monte, V. (2019). *Mom's Zucchini Bread* Recipe. Allrecipes. https://www.allrecipes.com/recipe/6698/moms-zucchini-bread/

NWMama. (n.d.). *Chewy French Baguette*. Allrecipes. https://www.allrecipes.com/recipe/272191/chewy-french-baguette/

Pammpurrd. (n.d.). *Clare's Whole Wheat Potato Bread*. Allrecipes. https://www.allrecipes.com/recipe/78291/clares-whole-wheat-potato-bread/

Parris, B. (n.d.). *Simple Milk Bread*. Allrecipes. https://www.allrecipes.com/recipe/257700/simple-milk-bread

PDPhotos. (2010, December 15). *Dough kneed hands – Free photo on Pixabay*. Pixabay. [Image]. https://pixabay.com/photos/dough-knead-hands-bake-ingredients-3468/

Pellegrinelli, C. *The Bread Making Equipment All Home Bakers Should Have*. The Spruce Eats. https://www.thespruceeats.com/necessary-equipment-for-baking-bread-303429

Pexels. (2016, October 23) *Two brown baked breads on table – Free stock photo*. [Image]. https://www.pexels.com/photo/baked-bread-breakfast-buns-209206/

Rose. (n.d.). *Best Ever Banana Bread*. Allrecipes. https://www.allrecipes.com/recipe/15747/best-ever-banana-bread/

Rosemary. (2018c, October 4). *Homemade Olive Oil Bread Rolls*. An Italian in My Kitchen. https://anitalianinmykitchen.com/olive-oil-bread/

Spearl. (n.d.). *Honey Oat Beer Bread*. Allrecipes. https://www.allrecipes.com/recipe/78095/honey-oat-beer-bread/

Spetnitskaya, N. (No date) *Person Making Dough Beside Brown Wooden Rolling Pin Photo*. Unsplash. [Image]. https://unsplash.com/photos/tOYiQxF9-Ys

Stafford, G. (2020, April 19). *The 7 Common Breadmaking Mistakes You're Probably Making*. Gemma's Bigger Bolder Baking. https://www.biggerbolderbaking.com/7-common-breadmaking-mistakes/.

Swalker3. (n.d.). *Gluten-Free Multigrain Bread*. Allrecipes. https://www.allrecipes.com/recipe/259323/gluten-free-multigrain-bread/

Ulleo. (2016, May 16). *Dough hand kneed – Free photo on Pixabay*. Pixabay. [Image]. https://pixabay.com/photos/dough-hand-knead-bake-bread-craft-1394214/

V. Malidate. (2017, December 6). *Person making dough – free stock photo*. Pexels. [Image]. https://www.pexels.com/photo/baked-baking-chef-dough-784633/

Van Buren, A. (2017, March 29. *The 12 Most Common Bread Baking Mistakes to Avoid*. MyRecipes. https://www.myrecipes.com/how-to/how-to-avoid-the-most-common-bread-baking-mistakes.

Webentwicklerin. (2020. March 16). *Toast white bread pastries – Free photo on Pixabay.* Pixabay. [Image]. https://pixabay.com/photos/toast-white-bread-pastries-fresh-4935132/

Welty, M. P. (n.d.). *Amazingly Easy Irish Soda Bread.* Allrecipes. https://www.allrecipes.com/recipe/16947/amazingly-easy-irish-soda-bread

Printed in Great Britain
by Amazon